REALISTIC ADVICE FOR
A HEALTHY ADOPTIVE FAMILY

THE WHOLE LIFE
ADOPTION
B · O · O · K

JAYNE E. SCHOOLER

PIÑON PRESS

P.O. Box 35007, Colorado Springs, Colorado 80935

OUR GUARANTEE TO YOU

We believe so strongly in the message of our books that we are making this quality guarantee to you. If for any reason you are disappointed with the content of this book, return the title page to us with your name and address and we will refund to you the list price of the book. To help us serve you better, please briefly describe why you were disappointed. Mail your refund request to: PiñonPress, P.O. Box 35002, Colorado Springs, CO 80935.

© 1993 by Jayne E. Schooler

All rights reserved. No part of this publication may be reproduced in any form without written permission from Piñon Press, P.O. Box 35007, Colorado Springs, CO 80935.

Library of Congress Catalog Card Number:
93-17998

ISBN 08910-97228

Some of the anecdotal illustrations in this book are true to life and are included with the permission of the persons involved. All other illustrations are composites of real situations, and any resemblance to people living or dead is coincidental.

Schooler, Jayne E.
      The whole life adoption book : realistic advice for
  building a healthy adoptive family / Jayne E. Schooler.
        p. cm.
     ISBN 0-89109-722-8
     1. Adoption.   2. Adoptive parents.
  I. Title.
  HV875.S365   1993
  362.7'34—dc20   93-17998
                                  CIP

Printed in the United States of America

7 8 9 10 / 05 04 03 02 01

Contents

To David,
my pastor, my husband, my best friend

Acknowledgments

From the first thought to the last word, I have learned that no book is written alone. Because many friends, colleagues, and family members cared enough to give words of encouragement and considerable assistance, this effort was completed. Although it is impossible to thank everyone who touched this project in some way, I would like to express my deep appreciation to the following:

To Dr. John Trent, who saw a need for this book and guided it into the hands of Piñon Press.

To my editor, Traci Mullins, for her continual words of encouragement and most competent direction.

To those special families who have shared their lives and stories.

To Otis and Dorothy Baty, whose financial gift enabled the purchase of a computer, an invaluable gift.

To Mrs. Chuck (Carol) Hamlin for her invaluable critiques from the very beginning of the dream.

To all my colleagues at Warren County Children Services, Lebanon, Ohio, for their encouragement to learn and grow in my job and for the support and flexibility in allowing me time to develop this manuscript—plus a special thank you to Mr. R. D. Burchwell, Executive Director; Mr. Steve Kelhoffer, Placement Supervisor; Mary Ann Martina (my first supervisor); and to those with whom I work most closely—Gwen Stuart, Joy Lovely, Pam Handley, Betsy Bingham, Jackie Wright, and Jeff Centers (who spent a year teaching me how to use the computer).

A special appreciation to two expressive colleagues whose "How's the book going?" provided needed motivation almost daily—Linda Smith and Celina Meyer.

To my most treasured friends at the Lebanon, Ohio, Church of the Nazarene who walked with me in the beginning of this project, and to my new and deeply valued friends at the West Carrollton, Ohio, Church of the Nazarene who encouraged me at the finish line.

I want to thank the two most important people of my household who sacrificed family time and carried additional responsibilities so that this book could be written: my most treasured source of friendship, encouragement, and support not only for this book but for all areas of my life—my husband, David; and my sixteen-year-old daughter, Kristy, who hopes to pursue a college degree in social work and psychology.

Finally, I am deeply grateful to God for providing such a tremendous opportunity and meeting a lifelong desire of my heart.

Introduction:
A Relationship of Promise

There are two kinds of relationships in life. One type of connection is genetic—such as the one we share with our birth parents, brothers, sisters, aunts, uncles, and our own birth children. No matter what happens, that tie always exists. Nothing can erase the permanency of the biological relationship.

The other kind is a union that begins with a promise. Marriage is such a union. Adoption is another. The adoption tie, established by the promise to act as a permanent family to a child born to another, mirrors that of a biological family in many ways. However, within that promise are dynamics that set it apart.

Excited adoptive parents often enter the relationship of promise with little perception of or adequate preparation for the unique challenges resident within adoption. Some of these issues follow all members of the adoption union, the parents and the child, throughout life. When issues that normally occur within the framework of adoption arise unexpectedly, parents can experience a wide range of unsettling reactions: guilt, a sense of failure, inadequacy, fear, or helplessness.

There are critical times in the life of most adoptive families when any one of a number of adoption-related matters presented in this book may surface. Without sensitive handling, these fragile concerns become painful, possibly even threatening the foundation of the adoption promise.

The purpose of this book is threefold:

- First, to acquaint prospective and new adoptive parents with the issues surrounding the early steps of the journey.
- Second, to validate the concerns of adoptive families in the middle of the child-rearing years who find themselves wondering if what they are experiencing is normal and how best to solve unexpected pressures and problems.
- Third, to offer direction to parents facing the crucial transitional years of adolescence and young adulthood.

This book has been written not only from the perspective gained through working with many adoptive families, but also from the heart of an adoptive parent. It is hoped that this effort will encourage families to take the journey into adoption with excitement and anticipation, bolstered by the knowledge and understanding that will create a happy, nurturing family environment.

PART ONE

Adoption: A Labor of the Heart

CHAPTER ONE

Choosing to Love a Stranger:
Unique Challenges Adoptive Parents Must Face

"Is she your real daughter?" they asked me.
"Real?" I questioned. "What do you mean by real?
She is a child not born of my flesh, that's true. But
she is a child truly born within my heart . . . within my soul.
Yes, she is real."
An adoptive mother

B rown-haired, brown-eyed, high-energy preschoolers Patrick and Lynne joined their family in 1986. The arrival of these affectionate youngsters ended years of waiting for Ron and Charlene Williams. After their first son was born, there was no hope for another child. They had always wanted a larger family. Now it was happening. They had become adoptive parents.

Kimberly was a severely neglected, malnourished foster child when she entered Bob and Debbie Jackson's home at three months old. For two-and-a-half years the Jacksons' desire to become Kimberly's permanent family grew with each passing month. Their hope teetered back and forth from court decision to court decision. After waiting twelve months for the decision of an appeals court, the word finally came. It was over. Kimberly was safe. She would stay with them. Bob and Debbie were adoptive parents.

Years of humiliating medical exams, endless questions, and emotional pain brought no hope to Tim and Traci Myatt. "You have unexplained infertility," doctors told them. "There is nothing else we can do for you medically." Today, four-year-old Timothy, born in Central America, steals the heart of everyone who meets him. Tim and Traci are also adoptive parents.

These families, along with thousands of families across this country, all have in common the choice they made to love, nurture, and train a stranger's child for a lifetime. It was a promise made to a genetically unrelated human being: "We want you to become one of us. We will be your family forever."

The events that brought these families to this common decision, however, are as different as are the families themselves.

For a majority of these couples, dreams of a household filled with the noisy, delightful confusion of children lay crushed by the distressing reality of infertility. For them, adoption was the very last hope for ever having a family.

For others, involvement in the temporary supervision of a child through a foster care program encouraged them to make a permanent home for the one they had grown to love.

Still others, already biological parents, felt called to open their home to an older child, thus assuming parenthood of an emotionally fragile child with the extra baggage of abuse, neglect, or abandonment.

In many ways, parenthood for adoptive couples is just like parenting a birth child. For the most part, the required skills overlap. However, from the inception of the adoption relationship, there are factors that set it apart. Without laying the proper groundwork in knowledge of these issues, parents who adopt can walk into their responsibilities without adequate understanding.

There are unique concerns affecting this relationship of promise. For example, families considering adoption must prepare differently for this distinctive parent-child relationship. Before the family takes the first step into the process they must decide that the journey into the adoption experience is a viable option for them. These preparations present challenges never faced within the biological experience. And then throughout the lifetime of the relationship between parent and child, unique dilemmas develop that demand direction. For these families, adoption is truly a labor of the heart.

MAKING THE DECISION TO ADOPT

Most couples think hard about the decision to take the first step toward adopting a child. Statistics indicate that it's usually about a year from the time a couple begins discussing adoption to making that first phone call. The idea emerges as a seed thought and appears to grow and gather energy.

It's important that before families involve themselves in the adoption process, they engage in a self-assessment of attitudes about themselves, their current situation, their current family life, and how they interface with their social environment.

Prospective adoptive parents can explore the following self-assessment questions with a spouse or trusted friend.

1. What are the reasons that I want to adopt?
2. How do I see adoption as a positive way to build my family?
3. In what ways do we have the kind of lifestyle and married life that will be enhanced by the addition of a new family member?
4. (Or) do we have personal problems that we think may improve if a child enters our family?
5. Is our motivation to adopt "to save a child"?
6. What is our perspective on the potential relationship — do we want a child for the parent, or are we a family for a child? In other words, what are our expectations for the child?
7. Are we adopting to acquire a playmate for our biological child?
8. Can we love and nurture this child without knowledge of his or her history?
9. Adoption is a team effort between parents, agencies, attorneys, and other individuals. How capable do we see ourselves of working through the system?
10. When we think of a child, what do we envision?
11. If infertility is an issue, what point of resolution have we reached regarding our inability to conceive?
12. If as a couple we have come to the realization that we

will never have birth children, how did the news make
us feel (as individuals and as a couple) when we first
heard it? Have we shared the depth of those emotions
with each other? Can we see the child to be adopted as
a resolution to childlessness?
13. How has infertility affected our marriage?
14. How has infertility affected my own self-concept?
15. How has childlessness affected my relationships with
relatives, friends, and their children?
16. Are we sufficiently content with our present circumstances so that we will avoid becoming obsessive
about adoption and narrowly focused while we wait to
become parents?

These questions may prove helpful in assessing a family's
readiness for the adoption experience. After a couple explores
their own outlook on adoption, the preparation can begin.

PREPARATION: CHARTING AN UNKNOWN COURSE

When Sam and Cynthia first contacted an agency because of their
interest in adoption, they had no knowledge of how to prepare
for the process. As they attended a training course, they became
familiar with five sensitive areas that set apart adoption readiness from birth parenting. Their new understanding enhanced
their own attitudes toward adoption and helped prepare them
for the uncertainties ahead.

INFERTILITY—THE STEALER OF DREAMS

When most young adults approach marriage, they assume that
at some point they will start a family. Most likely, in their child-
hoods they filled hours of playtime rehearsing mother and father
roles, projecting that someday in the future they too would be
just like Mom or Dad.

Disappointing for some, the assumption of this natural
course of events proves false. Infertility steals the dream.

Forced to face the reality of their situation, couples find
themselves coping with feelings and fears totally foreign to peers

loaded down with babies and diaper bags.

In a survey conducted several years ago but still relevant to the infertile couples of the 1990s, men and women provided emotionally penetrating responses to the following question: "There was once a time in your life when you wanted children, but could not have them. What word or words describe your feelings at that time?"[1]

Women, with a profound sense of hopelessness, responded that they felt "forlorn, unfulfilled, useless, absolutely heartsick, bitter, utterly desolate."

Men, projecting feelings similar to those of their wives, replied that they felt "disappointed, concerned for their wife's reaction, frustrated and inadequate."[2]

Tim and Traci lived under the shadow of unexplained infertility through four years of painful tests and procedures that shed no light on their circumstance. Chained to a calendar and thermometer that dictated the timing of their physical relationship, they felt trapped in a pursuit that had no end. Those circumstances nearly destroyed the joy and beauty God intended for them to experience in this dimension of their marriage.

"I can take you back to the hospital room where I made a decision," Tim commented. "As I stood beside Traci while she endured the pain of her sixth artificial insemination procedure, I knew right then and there—this was the last time. Four years on the roller coaster, hoping from month to month for a positive word, were enough. No more attempts at anything. We would have to change directions. We would have to struggle now with being childless or deciding what next steps to take in relation to adoption."

As the biological clock ticked away in the lives of Doug and Dorothy Hammon, their hope for a family diminished with each passing year. "I came from a family of seven children," Dorothy said. "Doug came from a family of five children. We loved large families and planned to follow the same course. I couldn't imagine anyone not being able to have a baby. It was beyond my belief that God would require that heartbreak of anyone."

"Involuntary childlessness" produces what adoption expert David Kirk calls a "role handicap." Couples motivated toward adoption by infertility enter parenthood from a different direction than they had expected. They have to alter their plans. Their expectations and needs for having children may overwhelm them emotionally, possibly blinding them to the realities inherent in the adoptive relationship.

Couples who view adoption as their last and desperate hope for a family face potentially major losses, especially in their expectations of themselves and what they perceive to be the expectations of others. Couples progressively face "the loss of oneself or one's partner as capable of conceiving a child, and the loss of the status of a biological parent and the presentation of a child to grandparents." And, of course, they face the most devastating loss of "the hoped-for birth child to carry on the family line."[3]

A primary challenge in preparing for the adoptive parent role is *to mourn the loss of the dream*. Couples should also realize that this loss may quietly follow them all their lives, subtly affecting their responses to their children in healthy as well as unhealthy ways. We'll explore all these issues more deeply in later chapters.

NO MODEL TO FOLLOW

Forced to change course, couples find themselves facing still other challenges and role handicaps in preparing for adoptive parenthood.

John and Marilyn Martin had finally decided that children would never be a part of their future unless they adopted. But they were troubled by the fact that they didn't know anyone who had taken this route. There was no one they could turn to for guidance. They needed answers for their questions but hesitated to keep calling the social worker, figuring that what was important to them would probably seem insignificant to her. So they didn't call.

Unlike birth parents, who are likely to have seen parenting modeled in their own experiences in their family of origin, "adoptive parents have little or no intimate contact with other adopters as *adoptive parents*."[4] They might not even know an adopted child. Most likely, they don't have anyone they can identify with whom they can bounce off feelings and concerns.

As David Kirk suggests, this presents a second major challenge in the preparation process: *Adoptive parents generally have no role models to steer them through the process.*

OUR BUSINESS IS NOT OUR OWN

In addition to the emotionally charged motivation to have a family, complicated by the lack of role models, couples entering the adoption journey lack a sense of privacy and control.

Birth parents are rarely subject to the personal scrutiny, decisions, and influences of others in the process of building a family. Adoptive parents have no choice. Each step of the way, they must seek direction from professionals in the field. They must walk through a network of intrusive examinations by outsiders, from social workers to court officials. They feel that they must monitor what they say and how they say it in fear that a trivial comment may disrupt the procedure.

These factors create a third concern during the preparation stage: *Adoptive parents soon begin to feel that their futures are out of their control. Their hopes and dreams are in the hands of strangers.*

THE WAIT CAN BE SO LONG

A fourth difficulty for adoptive applicants is the concept of time. When anticipating the arrival of a birth child, couples have a pretty good idea (usually within a few days or weeks) of when to plan for the event. Adoptive parents must wait indefinitely (so it seems) just to get on an agency list for a "homestudy." Then they must wade through a maze of paperwork and interviews during this process. Finally, once the procedure has been completed, the suspense *really* begins. Each ring of the phone may be the agency informing them of a child in need of a family.

When do couples tell their family and friends that they are adopting—when they first decide? Or during the homestudy? Or do they wait until they get the phone call? How can couples gather support around themselves when all they can answer to the when and who questions is "I don't know"?

Therefore, the fourth frustrating challenge in making the transition into adoptive parenthood is that *these expectant adults have no sense of a timetable. They have no clue how or when to prepare for the arrival of a new family member.*

SHARED PARENTING FOR A SEASON

Another obstacle in preparing for adoptive parenthood crops up immediately after the child arrives: the question of parental rights over the newest child in the home. When are adoptive parents really the parents? On the day of arrival? Physically, yes. Legally, no. The child still remains in the legal custody of the birth parent, an agency, or the court. A social worker and/or court worker will regularly visit the home for a period of six months prior to finalization.

These visits are a constant reminder of how different adoptive parenting is. For the child's best interest, parental status is not fully granted in most states until that trial period expires. And so a fifth and final test for adoptive parents as they enter their new role is that *they must cope with the lack of full entitlement as parents while functioning in the position as if they were.*

Pre-adoptive families who realize that they must prepare for their role differently than do birth parents will be more successful in managing the uncertainties that are a natural course of events. They will be better prepared for encountering adoption's four unique dilemmas, which will be introduced in this first chapter. The rest of this book will explore the adoptive family relationship in depth and give practical guidelines for dealing with the challenges.

The unique dilemmas of adoption center around the fact that parental rights and obligations may be transferred but shared genetic descent cannot be. It is most important that during the pre-adoptive stage, parents begin to understand the realities of the relationship they are entering. It is equally important that parents in the midst of the parenting task stand back and evaluate how they have approached the unique dilemmas of adoptive parenting.

DILEMMA NUMBER ONE: HOW DO WE SEE OUR FAMILY?

Joe and Gayle Smith and Robert and Joyce Bennett had something in common. They had waited for five years for that all-important phone call from the private adoption agency serving them. Within two months of each other, the calls finally came. For both couples, the waiting was over.

Three-week-old John joined the Smith family immediately. Within two years, Alicia, a month-old infant, completed the family circle. That was over twenty-one years ago. To this day, both children (now, of course, young adults) have no idea that they were adopted. Gayle and her husband decided that their family was "just like anyone else's." They decided to "forget" the children were not theirs by birth and to build the relationship from that perspective.

The Bennett family approached the adoption relationship very differently. Almost from the moment that two-week-old June captured the hearts of her waiting parents, the Bennetts communicated her special position in the family. Now an adult, June says of her parents' conversation about adoption,

> They told me that even from the time I was in the cradle, they would talk to me about adoption. They would say things like, "We wanted a baby so badly; we are so fortunate to have you." They would always say how much they loved me. There was never a time that my parents had to sit me down and tell me I was adopted. I always knew it. It was just built in as part of our relationship.

Note the dissimilarity between these two approaches. The Smiths chose to permanently "reject the differences" that are a normal and natural part of adoption.[5] This plan would meet their need to lessen the sting of infertility and be just like everyone else. The strategy would work—for a while. The consequences of such a perspective would not be felt for years to come.

The Bennetts, on the other hand, embraced the reality of their role in their daughter's life and "acknowledged the differences." They had reconciled their fertility deprivation and arrived at a healthy understanding of their current role. They were able to say, "Yes, we are different; nevertheless we ARE a family." Adoptive parents must learn the delicate balance between denying the difference in the nurturing process and acknowledging it in communicating to the child about his or her past. (This dilemma is more fully examined in chapter 7.)

DILEMMA NUMBER TWO: HOW DO WE DEVELOP A NURTURING RELATIONSHIP?

When birth children arrive in a family, just like adopted children, they are "strangers" who seek to be accepted for who they are. However, by the very nature of their appearance on the scene, most birth children are more easily incorporated into the family—physically, emotionally, and psychologically. The same needs for blending into the family exist for adopted children, but a heavier assignment is added to the parents' responsibilities.

Goal one of parenting is to accept and know each child. Goal two is to incorporate or integrate children into the family. Creating an environment in which children feel secure and loved enables them to move on. Parents then begin the third assignment of parenting: developing secure, autonomous children. They must help their children to differentiate from their family of origin.

This third goal does not begin in the early stages of the relationship. Newborns and toddlers are completely dependent upon their parents for total survival, and trust and interdependence are developed during this stage. Separation begins as children develop and mature. The first hints of differentiating start as children move out first into their neighborhood, then on into preschool and beyond. Their ability to function well outside the home is determined largely by the quality of attachment and sense of belonging they experience early on in their home.

The adoptive parents' position in this new assignment is like the birth parents'—to integrate the new child into the family. But the similarity ends there, for from the beginning of the adoptive relationship these same adults are "expected to engage in differentiating acts practically from the start."[6] These very differentiating acts, so important for honest communication, may possibly affect the depth of attachment a family is able to achieve.

Even before the family has had time to form deep attachments with the child, they are told to begin communicating the difference. Integrate the child into the home, they are told. Make sure the difference is articulated from the beginning, they are counseled. But this task is laden with emotional conflicts, as we will explore later in greater depth (see section 2 and chapter 9).

DILEMMA NUMBER THREE:
WHAT DO WE NEED TO KNOW ABOUT OUR CHILD,
AND WHAT SHOULD WE DO WITH WHAT WE KNOW?

When infants join their new family, most agencies make sincere efforts to obtain social and medical history about their family of origin. Although this is sometimes non-identifying information, it gives parents something of a handle on anticipating future talents and strengths as well as behavioral, educational, or medical problems that might be related to genetics.

When older children with histories of their own enter their adoptive families, parents are given information not only about the birth family, but also about the social, medical, psychological, and educational history of their child. This material allows potential adoptive parents to make realistic decisions concerning the child. Some parents fail to realize that it is in everyone's best interest and their right as parents to gather as much information about their child as possible.

David and Jennifer Dotson were determined to adopt. As far as they were concerned, they could handle any problems a child might have. They knew that love would conquer all. They just wanted a child — any child.

When they went into the agency for an interview concerning a possible child for their family, they went in with blinders on. They asked no questions. They explored no possible problems. They failed to hold the agency accountable to give them all the information it had available. In fact, they declined to read some very important medical information about their child.

Birth parents question a doctor from the first moment of a child's life. But adoptive parents often hesitate to assert themselves when presented with a child in need of adoption, for several reasons. They feel inadequate. They don't know what to ask. They grope along in darkness because they don't believe they are entitled to any information. They may be influenced by others to assume that they should simply be grateful for the opportunity and avoid rocking the boat.

However, parents have a right to know about their child's genetic potential and history. The child, in turn, will some day need to have that information passed on to him or her. (See chapter 8 for a full exploration of this dilemma.)

DILEMMA NUMBER FOUR: HOW DO WE FEEL ABOUT OUR CHILD'S BIRTH FAMILY?

For years, statistics have told us that more and more children are born to unwed mothers who could be carriers of venereal disease or addicted to drugs. Child abuse and the subsequent termination of parental rights among these parents is also increasing dramatically. Both situations plunge innocent youngsters into the adoption arena.

Parents who adopt confront a fourth dilemma. They must face their feelings about their child's history, racial and cultural ties, and birth family. They must acknowledge the possibility of genetic liabilities, drugs, alcohol, and venereal disease. They must reconcile their attitudes toward these realities in light of their own value structure. Finally, they must recognize that such a negative beginning can have far-reaching consequences for the child (through behavior and/or infirmities) and for themselves (in their ultimate ability to accept the child fully). Adoptive parents must decide how, when, and how much of the truth of those circumstances they will communicate to the child, knowing that an adopted child's self-esteem can be affected by his or her perceptions of genetic origins. (This dilemma is addressed in chapters 8 and 12.)

Adoption is truly a labor of the heart—and head! It begins with a time of difficult preparation. It is filtered through months, even years, of process. By its very nature, adoption carries with it lifelong dilemmas that potentially can dictate success or failure.

SUMMARY

Adoptive parents enter adoption with five major challenges unique to preparing for this experience.
First, they may have to mourn the loss of their dream — their ability to conceive children, their status as birth parents, and their birth child.

Second, they are unlikely to have role models for guiding them through the process.

Third, they must realize that their hope for a family will be dictated by the input of strangers.

Fourth, pre-adoptive parents have no timetable by which to plan their future.

Fifth, parental rights are not fully granted for at least six months into the relationship.

Parents will face a lifetime of dilemmas that are characteristic only of the adoptive family relationship.
1. "How do we see our family?" Do we acknowledge or deny the difference?

2. "How do we build a nurturing relationship?" When and how do we begin to communicate the difference to our adopted child?

3. "What do we need to know about our child, and what should we do with what we know?" How do we get important facts about our child's past? When do we communicate those facts?

4. "How do we feel about our child's birth family?" How do we reconcile our child's beginnings with our own value system, and how do we relate this to the child without a negative attitude?

QUESTIONS FOR SMALL GROUPS

1. What particular challenges have you had in preparing to become an adoptive family?

2. If infertility has been an issue, what problems has it created within you, within your marriage, and with your relationships with couples who have children?

3. How have you handled your infertility in relation to your hopes and your personal faith? In what ways have you worked through bitterness, anger at God, feelings of inadequacy, and so forth?

4. What are your needs and expectations of yourself, of your spouse, and of the agency with which you work?

5. If you are an experienced adoptive parent, can you relate to the four dilemmas of adoption? Can you think of any others?

CHAPTER TWO

Creating a Family:

How Do Children Enter Our Homes, and Who Are They?

*When Catherine first came, it seemed impossible to me that any child
wouldn't respond to a warm and nurturing home.
As I learned to watch her and understand her pain,
I knew beneath that hardened shell was a child trying desperately
to feel and to love again.*
Cynthia, an adoptive parent

J eff and Gwen Stewart had planned a week together at the beach.
One phone call from their attorney changed everything. "Mr.
and Mrs. Stewart, this is Mr. Barrett. We have just received word
that your baby's arrival will come sooner than expected. Instead
of three more weeks, it could happen any day. I suggest that you
not leave town." They canceled their vacation plans.

The Stewarts joined hundreds of families waiting each day for
a phone call or home visit to bring their deepest desire to reality. Like many prospective adoptive parents, Jeff and Gwen went
through a preparation period, not only formally through classes but
also emotionally, psychologically, and spiritually. They emerged
ready to walk through the process of adoption best suited for them.

THE PROCESS: ADOPTION'S MANY OPTIONS

When a family decides to pursue adoption, there are several
avenues they can explore. Each option, however, requires a home-

study: a thorough examination of the home, the quality of relationships, financial security, motivation, and lifestyle. The depth of the process varies from agency to agency.

PUBLIC AGENCY ADOPTIONS

Public agencies are run by either state or county governments. Children are without question legally freed for adoption prior to placement. Many public agencies do not charge a fee. When an older child or sibling group adoption is arranged, state and federal financial subsidies often are available to the family to help with ongoing expenses for medical or psychological care. Even legal expenses are reimbursable in many states.

Waiting lists for very young children are generally very long. Families who are interested in adopting children over the age of three are given a higher priority in homestudy completion. Many states have initiated a foster-to-adopt program since it's in the child's best interest to avoid multiple moves.

There are generally two routes into adoption with public agencies: direct agency adoption and foster care adoption.

Direct Agency Adoption

One Sunday morning, Charlene Williams walked by the church nursery and glanced in at the children. She caught sight of a little fellow sitting alone whose sad eyes cried out for someone to notice him.

Charlene heard that three-year-old Patrick and his two-year-old sister Lynne were living in a foster home. Her heart went out to the children. She wanted to gather them in her arms. Little did she know that a short time later, these two children would be walking into her home, on the way to becoming her son and daughter.

The Williams began their adoption journey in 1977. Following two miscarriages and a pessimistic outlook for a birth child, they decided to adopt. They contacted the local public children services agency and began the homestudy process. They finished the requirements and sat back anxiously to wait. Two years passed with no word from the agency.

While they were waiting, something happened that put their

adoption plans on hold. In 1980, "their miracle," son Robbie, was born, and they decided to postpone adoption. Five years later, their desire to adopt resurfaced and they contacted the local public agency to let them know of their renewed interest. It turned out to be perfect timing.

One rainy March morning in 1986, just a few months after the Williams had re-initiated the procedure, they received a phone call. "Would you be interested in discussing the adoptive placement of two preschoolers?" Upon hearing a brief description of the children, Charlene realized that they were the same youngsters who had tugged at her heart just weeks before. Her new family was right under her nose.

Patrick and his little sister came for pre-placement visits to get to know their new family. They moved into their new home on Easter weekend, 1986. Following a six-month waiting period, the family filed for the legal adoption in court to make the children a permanent part of the family.

In the summer of 1991, the family jointly made the decision to adopt again. All three children, Rob (age twelve), Patrick (ten), and Lynne (nine), were excited about opening their hearts and home to four-year-old Stephanie.

Foster Care Adoption

Bob and Debbie Jackson had no intention of becoming adoptive parents when they entered the foster care program of the local children's services agency. The parents of two daughters who were heading into the preteen years, the Jacksons wanted to open their home to help an abused child only for a little while. What they had not counted on was falling in love with Kimberly.

Kimberly, now age five, came to live with the Jacksons at the age of three months. When she was brought to their door by the agency social worker, she was severely malnourished, desperately dirty, and lethargic. Weeks of tender care and nurture brought color and life back to the child. The Jacksons' job was to work as members of the agency team in helping Kimberly's mother do a better job of caring for her.

Debbie commented:

As we cared for this little girl, our lives and futures were
on hold. Each week, we would take her to visit her birth
mother. Sometimes she would stay overnight. Kimberly
would always cry when we left her there. She didn't
understand who this person was. When she would return
home, we had to deal with tantrums, sleeplessness, and
eating problems for several days. Just as she settled back
down, it was time for a visit again.

We were advised not to become too attached. But how
could a small child feel secure if we withheld affection
from her? If we kept our distance, it would be easier for
us — but devastating to her. So we loved.

As the months passed, we began to feel that she was
one of us — but of course, she wasn't. We wanted to map
out a design to enlarge our home if she stayed, but there
were no assurances of that. We wanted to plan a family
vacation, but were uncertain where to go. If Kimberly
was with us in the summer, we wouldn't plan a water
park trip.

There were times I would become so angry! We were
doing so much for this little girl, and it seemed that her
neglectful mother ran the program. I had to believe that
God had Kimberly's best interests in mind far more than
even we did.

Over an eighteen-month period, the weekly visits with
Kimberly's mother failed to bring improvement. The emotional
ups and downs for this family seemed to end with a court order
terminating parental rights. However, the birth mother appealed
the lower court decision and the final outcome was postponed
for another fourteen months.

After caring for this child for over two-and-a-half years, the
Jacksons received the word. It was finally over. What began as a
temporary desire on the part of a family to make a difference in
their world had turned into a permanent commitment. Following
the termination of parental rights, the Jackson family applied to
the public agency to be approved as adoptive parents. Kimberly's
future was secure.

INTERCOUNTRY ADOPTION

Parents choosing to adopt a child from another country most often will be involved with at least two agencies. First, the couple is required to work with an agency in this country to complete an initial homestudy and paperwork. Following that process, the family's file is sent to an overseas agency, which refers children to waiting families. Exceptions to this procedure are possible, but they must be carefully screened.

Depending upon the country, the wait can be from six months to well over a year. As soon as a child is matched with a family, paperwork including visas, passports, immigration applications, and other essential documents must be gathered.

Just as Tim and Traci Myatt had laid aside the dreams of having a family, a dramatic series of events reignited their hope.

"When we made the decision to adopt," Tim recalled, "we really didn't know how to go about it. We went to see a pastor we knew who had helped other families. We figured he would direct us toward adoption in this country. Instead, he encouraged us to meet with another couple who had recently arrived home from Guatemala with their adopted infant son."

Interestingly, Tim had just returned from a church-sponsored trip to that same country. While there, his assignment was to work in an orphanage. He quickly fell in love with the Guatemalan youngsters.

When Tim and Traci drove to another part of their state to consult with the adoptive couple, they had a growing sense that perhaps this was the first step toward starting a family. The Pages told the Myatts the procedure for adopting a child directly from Guatemala, suggesting that they contact the same Guatemalan lawyer with whom they had worked.

Tim immediately returned home and wrote a lengthy letter of introduction and application to the attorney. More than a month passed before they heard anything. Then a return letter arrived.

Traci recalled:

The letter said, "It is to people like you that we wish to extend the service of adoption." It was their way of saying, we will sponsor you in this country, we will be your attorney. This letter outlined the documentation we would need to provide. It was our first ray of hope.

During the following months Tim and Traci spent hours writing extensive autobiographies and gathering thorough references and other complicated documents. All their paperwork had to be funneled through the Guatemalan consulate in this country.

Finally, anticipation turned into reality when the Myatts were informed that they were matched with a baby boy. They were given instructions to prepare to leave for Guatemala. They were to spend two weeks in the country with their new son before he would be eligible to leave.

One Thursday evening in March 1989, thirteen months after they had started the process, the phone rang. It was their Central American attorney. He told them to make plans to leave for his country the following Wednesday. Their son was waiting for them.

Bright, spirited Timothy Justin had been born in October 1988. He was placed into the Myatts' arms in March 1989. Traci reflected on the events that brought their son to them:

> When we went to see the Pages in Cleveland, it was almost to the day that Justin was conceived. There were periods of great apprehension. Would this fall through? We knew we were involved in an incredible risk. Anything could happen. The country could turn us down when we got there. The mother could change her mind. Our son might be too ill to leave. It was one of the most dramatic periods in our lives in which we had to place our faith totally in God, day by day.

INDEPENDENT ADOPTION

Considered the most risky option for adoption success, independent adoptions are most often arranged by either a doctor or an attorney. These individuals develop a network of families seeking adoption and match these couples with birth mothers who wish to plan an adoption for their child. Attorneys also handle private adoptions arranged by families. Costs for this type of adoption can be excessively high, depending on how it is handled.

Independent adoption is illegal in three states: North Dakota, Michigan, and Delaware. In Connecticut and Massachusetts, families can locate a birth mother, but state agencies must oversee the entire arrangement.[1]

A Risk for Love

Dear Doug and Dorothy,
I wanted to keep you informed on how I am doing. I went to the clinic last week. The doctor said that I had gained weight, but that was to be expected at this point in the pregnancy. He listened to the baby's heartbeat and everything sounds just fine. He thinks that the baby is due October 21. That means we only have two more months. My parents will call you as agreed so that you can be with us in the delivery room. Thank you for being willing to love my baby.
I'll write again soon,
Patti

For Doug and Dorothy Hammon, that letter and earlier contacts represented their only prospect for a family. Each short note from the birth mother of their prospective child brought them closer to the fulfillment of their deepest desire—to have a family.

The Hammons spent seven years and thousands of dollars looking for an answer to their infertility problem. When Dorothy turned thirty-five, they decided that adoption was their only option for a family.

Dorothy commented:

I began making calls to public and private agencies. They wouldn't even put our names on the waiting list. The prospects for a healthy white infant were bleak.
One afternoon Doug's boss walked into his office and

shut the door. He related that the fifteen-year-old daughter of a friend of his was pregnant and the family wanted to have the child adopted by a good family. He asked if we would be interested.

When Doug called me at home, for the first time in a very long time, I felt that we had a chance to add a child to our family.

During the next several months, the Hammons and the teenage birth mother and her family spent time together in their respective homes. Patti keep the family regularly informed through letters or phone calls. Both families obtained lawyers, and the Hammons agreed to pay all legal expenses. Patti's medical expenses were covered on her parents' health insurance policies.

Finally, in early November 1985 the Hammons received the long-awaited call. Patti was on the way to the hospital. Because of the openness of the adoption both families accepted, Doug and Dorothy were in the delivery room at the time of their son's birth. Within one hour after his arrival, Dorothy held him in her arms.

"In that moment," Dorothy recalled, "I felt overwhelmed with thanksgiving. I was totally awed."

The next few days were difficult for this waiting family. They left the hospital the evening after the birth so that Patti and her family could spend time with the baby. They knew that at any moment, Patti could change her mind—for up to fifteen days *after* the baby joined his adoptive family. However, happily for Doug and Dorothy, she did not.

Jamie is now six years old. The Hammons send yearly updates to his birth mother and talk with her, usually at Christmas time. A deep desire of the heart has been fulfilled.

❖ ❖ ❖

Each one of these families walked through a lengthy procedure to adopt. Some adopted infants. Others experienced the joys and challenges of adopting older children. But at whatever age children become part of an adopting family, they come with their own unique needs and strengths. Just who are the children who become ours?

WHO ARE THE CHILDREN WHO ENTER OUR HOMES?

Sharon slipped down to the basement to switch the last load of laundry to the dryer. She was glad that her husband had left to run errands and that four-year-old Kelly was asleep. She needed time alone to sort through her emotions.

She and Greg had worked hard in preparing for Kelly to come live with them. They had attended classes, talked with other adoptive parents, and read quite a lot. They thought they were adequately prepared. Yet Sharon felt extremely guilty. All day long she had kept asking herself, *What am I doing wrong? This isn't what I expected. Are we going to make it? Adoptive parents shouldn't feel this way.*

Kelly was a beautiful, energetic three-year-old when she entered their home five months earlier. The agency that arranged the adoption had given Sharon and Greg some information about her past: Kelly was a victim of extreme neglect, a typical "failure to thrive" infant. She had been placed into foster care on two different occasions but both times returned to her birth parents.

Finally, at age three Kelly was removed permanently then placed into their family. This bright youngster brought with her unreported behavioral problems: aggression and self-abusive conduct. She would not allow Sharon to hug her or even hold her hand. Sharon knew that children even as young as Kelly could have problems. But she hadn't known what it was like to live with them day after day.

Adoption creates a delicate relationship. It can be profoundly challenging to assume a parental role for an infant whose details of genetics and family background are for the most part secret. It presents significant demands on a mother figure to effectively guide a growing child with pressing emotional needs—a child with whom a woman has no history of enjoyment or fulfillment. It is a sensitive test to become a father figure for a child for whom a man has no sense of entitlement—the indisputable belonging to one another.[2]

For adoptive parents such as Sharon and Greg Turner, sustaining "the promise" will require two very important steps: honestly facing the realities of adoption and choosing to react responsibly to those realities.

When adopting an infant, parents must be aware of the role of genetics in forming the personality and character development of a child. When adopting a child with a previous history in the birth home, even a toddler, parents must take into account not only the genetic factors but also the background from which their child has come. They must attempt to learn how that child coped within that dysfunctional family system.

Parents can better build a healthy family environment by examining the complete picture of genetic factors and first home experiences. Through incorporating several principles into their parenting skills—many of which are unique to adoption—these parents can manage their own reactions, feelings, and attitudes when the challenges come.

INFANT ADOPTION—WHAT ARE THE GENETIC GIVENS?

Every child who becomes part of an adoptive family comes with a pre-set genetic package. That genetic code dictates far more than the hair and eye color or height and weight. According to researchers, genetics play a highly instrumental role in the development of intelligence, temperament, artistic talents, and even career choices.

A newborn child is not a blank slate waiting to be written on with environmental influences. Rather, at the core of many of the behaviors and personality traits children exhibit are genetic ingredients that contribute to the development of a shy child or an extroverted one.

Often, genetic influences are considered only in relation to looks and intelligence capabilities. But studies show these are not the only areas affected:

> Genetics contribute not just to the grand total IQ scores, but also to more subtle patterns of ability: special talents for music, abstract reasoning, mechanical aptitudes, fine eye-hand coordination, spatial visualization.[3]

Parents must recognized that biologically determined differences in personality and intellect will greatly influence their child's interest, values, and temperament.

Dismissing the cloak of secrecy shrouding adoptions in earlier years, adoption agencies now attempt to collect as much information from the birth parents as feasible. Lengthy social and medical history interviews are conducted when possible to obtain not just a medical background but also a sketch of the interests, educational backgrounds, and abilities of the birth family.

Marietta Spencer, a social worker from Children's Society of Minnesota, commented, "a genetic history — psychological as well as medical — is something like a child's washing instructions. When you buy a sweater, you want to know all about its fabric content and how to take care of it. How much more important is it for you to know everything you can about the care of the child you are about to nurture?"[4]

Dan was just six months old when he was adopted into the James family. David and Catherine already had two birth sons. Dan was five years younger than their youngest child. As the children matured, the differences among them became obvious. Dan was taller and stronger than Matt and Joe. The James' birth children were both studious, quiet, and musically talented. They were following the unwritten rules that in order to be accepted in this home, everyone does well in school, studies hard, and masters a musical instrument.

Dan's lack of interest in both school and music was viewed by his parents as undesirable, almost unthinkable. They refused to allow him to pursue his strong interest in sports. Matt and Joe never played on Little League teams; so Dan didn't need to either.

By failing to unwrap the crucial genetic package Dan carried into their home, David and Catherine James widened the differences in the relationship. Their expectations for Dan would never be fulfilled. By the time he left home at eighteen, he felt inadequate and inept. Worst of all, he felt that he belonged nowhere.

When Dan turned twenty-two, he made a decision to find out about his birth parents. Although he could not obtain identifying information, he received details that brought a sense of continuity to his life. The letter that he received included a brief description of his birth father:

Your father was eighteen years old at the time of your birth. He was tall with dark brown hair and eyes. He was an average to below-average student. His strong interests included sports, both football and baseball.

For the first time in his life, Dan realized that he would not be inadequate or inept in another's eyes. He was just like his birth father. Although he never met him, he felt that he finally belonged somewhere, without prior conditions.

Facing the issue of genetics and relationship development encourages adoptive parents to assume two tasks. The first task is to tune into the child's "wavelength": "The lesser degree of parent-child similarities makes it harder for the adoptive parents to get on the child's wavelength—to see the world as the child does and to understand what makes the child tick."[5] Parents can work at attaining a discerning and empathetic style of interaction in which they listen beyond the words a child speaks and the behaviors he or she exhibits. The challenge continues to grow as the child grows and displays more of his or her own particular bent.

The second task for parents related to genetics and adopted children is to be willing to acknowledge those differences, support them, and accept them as part of the child's God-given design. The decision to recognize that each child is wonderfully unique and intrinsically valuable will sturdily prop open those important doors of communication so necessary for healthy development.

OLDER CHILD ADOPTIONS— WHAT DO THEY BRING WITH THEM?

Jenny, a victim of extreme abuse and multiple foster home placements, is finally being adopted. She was one of thirty-six thousand kids with special needs waiting for a permanent family in any given year—physically or mentally handicapped and older children dreaming of a "forever family." Jenny is now fortunate to be one of the twelve thousand children each year who will find that dream.

Before children like Jenny are adopted, however, they have

learned how to do something that dictates their response to life's stresses, pressures, and relationships: *survive.*

Most older children who enter adoptive families come from dysfunctional and chaotic families of origin. Nothing seemed to work well in their birth homes, whether it was holding a job or maintaining even a decent level of communication. Habitual drug or alcohol abuse usually plagued the home. At best, these children began life in homes where they lived as pinballs, bouncing off unaware and unattached. At worst, these children were victims of physical and sexual abuse that left lifelong scars. As their home became unfit, they were possibly shuttled between birth parents and foster homes, experiencing one relationship loss after another.

These are the conditions from which children enter the adoptive setting. Packed along with their belongings are behavioral coping skills they mastered in their birth families. They learned the rules. Don't talk. Don't trust. Don't feel.[6]

For older adopted children, life experiences have often stolen their sense of personal value. Their interactions with troubled parents who have been inconsistent or cruel have damaged their ability to love and respect themselves. They face life from these negative perceptions of themselves and of the world.

The coping mechanisms that these children have developed to confront the reality they see are deeply entrenched in their behavior. That's because these strategies represent security, freedom from pain, and control over their environment.[7]

These children assumed a specific role in the family as they developed coping mechanisms to survive at home. They carry that deeply ingrained role into the foster home, and they will carry it into the adoptive family (see table 2.1, page 40).

ALICIA — THE COMPETENT CHILD
Alicia is one of those unusual children. Kathy, her adoptive mother, rarely if ever has to tell her to make her bed, set the table, or run the vacuum. She just does it.

At thirteen, Alicia is the oldest of four children, all of whom are part of the same adoptive family. Alicia takes initiative in caring for her brothers and sister, often preempting Kathy's mothering efforts. She even takes the blame if one of them misbehaves.

Early in her young life, Alicia detected that if she and her siblings were to survive, she would have to do all she could to make it happen. Her first parents, both chained to alcohol and drug habits, often left her in charge of her siblings. By age five, Alicia was feeding babies and changing diapers. By age nine, when her birth mother was too drunk to get off the couch, it was her responsibility to get everyone off to school. Once school was out, Alicia hurried home to await the other children. She never knew if her parents would be there or if there would be anything to eat. She never talked about her home life to anyone.

Table 2.1: Patterns of Interaction that Move with the Child
from the Birth Home to the Adoptive Home*

---

1. Dysfunctional family rules: Don't talk, don't trust, don't feel.

2. Child attempts to build attachment to family by trying to follow rules.

3. Child's needs go unmet because he is unable to process his dysfunctional family system. He begins to shut down emotionally to avoid pain. A coping style emerges.

4. The child refines this coping style as the absence of pain reinforces his behavior. Soon a role in the family emerges.

5. This learned role may determine how he will attempt to build the new relationships in the adoptive home.

6. Adoptive parents who create an environment in which a child can learn what it is like to feel safe and secure and to trust can interrupt what could have been a lifetime of dysfunctional living.

---

*This chart was adapted from "Passing the Torch: The Multigenerational Transmission Process" by David Carder, found in *Secrets of Your Family Tree*. Used by permission.

Alicia's role in her family of origin was that of the competent child. She became the parent to her brothers and sister. As long as she worked hard at managing the home and family, she and the others would be safe. It was her obligation.

To her teachers and other adults in her world, Alicia appeared strong and happy. But on the inside she was empty and scared. She knew she couldn't mess up. She just had to remain capable.

Because these survival traits were so deeply a part of Alicia, she brought them along into the unknown and untried environment of her adoptive family. As her new parents grew to understand Alicia and to respond to her fears, it became a delight to watch the burden lift from her shoulders. The more secure this young girl became, the less she acted as "parent" to her siblings.

Her adoptive mom, Kathy, said, "I didn't think I would ever say I was glad to see a messy room, but the day I walked into Alicia's room and saw the clutter, it was just like a normal teen's world. We had passed through a difficult time. We are parenting a teenager now, nothing more, nothing less."

JULIA — THE WITHDRAWN CHILD

Unlike Alicia's outgoing demeanor, Julia, age seven, kept to herself. She was quiet, well-behaved, and withdrawn. Before entering the foster care system at age five, Julia lived in an abusive family. Although she was never physically abused by her alcoholic father, she witnessed many occasions of extremely harsh punishment directed at her brothers. The only words focused at her by her father were "get out of the way, stupid," or "you are such a bother." Finally, both parents abandoned the children.

Although Julia spent a brief five years in her family of origin, she had already chosen her pattern of coping with relationships. She would become the "lost child." As long as she stayed out of the way, no one would bother her. Her fears drove her into an emotional cavern. Any attempts to leave that safe environment brought pain and heartache. For her, surviving in a family meant retreating.

As Julia walked through the door of her new home, she dragged along her perception of family living: Don't talk and keep to yourself. Then you will be safe.

Julia's new parents prepared well for her arrival. They learned as much detail about her and her family of origin as they could. Because of that knowledge, they eased quietly into the relationship with Julia.

As time progressed Julia learned she was safe, secure, and

could trust these new people in her world. She slowly emerged from her cave. Today, the chattering youngster who waltzes into the kitchen after school bears little resemblance to the solemn child of two years earlier.

BILLY—THE BULLY

"Mrs. Richardson, Billy started a fight at recess today. It was his second confrontation of the day. He is sitting in the principal's office."

For Sue, this call was not unexpected. Billy, their newly adopted eight-year-old, had clashed with the other children in their home all week. It was just a matter of time before he took his behavior to school with him.

Billy is the bully. Before coming to the Richardsons' home, he lived with his birth parents. In that highly conflictive environment, no one communicated without screaming. If screaming didn't work, getting slapped around was next. That applied to everyone, from Billy's mom to his little brother. Billy had no idea what normal family living was like. He only knew what role he played.

Because Billy was more vocal than the rest of his siblings, he became the family target. He was a defiant rebel even at his young age. He craved attention, and negative attention was better than no attention. His aggressive temper got him just what he wanted.

Billy is the type of child who has a hypersensitive defense system and is quick to act, hurting people, pets, or things in the process. He can drain the energy from unprepared adoptive parents who soon find they can't tolerate living with this disruptive personality.

But Billy met his match in his new adoptive parents. He was the third adopted son of Sue and Gary Richardson. They knew children like Billy inside and out. They knew that deep inside that insubordinate youngster was a child. When Gary got home, all three of them would have a talk. It was time to begin family counseling, the caseworker suggested. They were looking forward to loving and guiding this child through his pain into a bright future.

ALLEN — THE MANIPULATOR

Allen joined his adoptive family at the age of ten. He arrived at the Carters' home with a smile and handshake for everyone. Even at that young age, he knew how to win people over. Allen's role in his family of origin was that of a manipulator.

Skilled at knowing how to work his way through the dysfunctional family system, Allen had discovered what worked — lies and deception. He could twist any story, shade any truth, tell any lie without a twinge of conscience. He could slip out of the range of his abusive birth father with a narrative so realistic it was never questioned. He knew what to say to make himself look good, and he said it.

Before long, Allen lost the ability to tell truth from fiction. It took some time for his new family to discover his ways, for they too bought his stories. He had won them over with his innocent manner. But it proved to be nothing but a facade.

As Allen's adoptive family learned positive ways to confront his lies with consequences while at the same time building his sense of security, they noticed that his negative behavior lessened. Allen still has a few more steps to take, but his parents feel a great sense of satisfaction in interrupting such a profound problem in the life of their son.

CHRISTOPHER — THE COMPLIANT CHILD

"Don't say anything. Just act as if it doesn't matter." How many times did Chris hear that from his mother, especially when his demanding father stumbled through the kitchen to get another beer?

By age seven, Chris had absorbed his mother's fears. He took on the role of the conforming child. As an abnormally compliant youngster, he learned that survival meant silence. He knew he must follow the dysfunctional rules to the letter — don't express any complaints, needs, or feelings.

On the outside, Chris appeared easygoing. That is exactly how a social worker described him. However, he carried with him into his new adoptive family, stuffed deep into his heart and mind, hidden rage. No one would have guessed it, for no one knew what he felt or thought. Chris really didn't either. He had learned that he wasn't supposed to think or feel. If he did it brought pain.

One of the first steps that Chris's new parents took was to model healthy family communication. They expressed their feelings to each other, spoke honestly to each other, and disagreed agreeably.

As Chris watched this loving family, the umbrella of security and protection opened over him. He gradually internalized those positive feelings and began to open up to his family.

Carl, his adoptive father, was thrilled when Chris began to express his own needs:

> One afternoon, I told Chris that it was time to come in.
> He would usually jump up and run into the house with
> no comment. But that day we had a breakthrough. He first
> stuttered around, not knowing how I would take it. Then
> he said, "I'm not ready yet. Can I stay a little longer?"
> That probably seems small and even silly. But it was the
> first time he *ever* said anything contrary to what he had
> been asked to do. We knew then the wall was beginning to
> crumble.

ALEX—THE PECULIAR CHILD

Alex wasn't like other kids. He was odd. No one liked him or wanted to be around him. Alex sat in class and made funny noises and said obnoxious things. Everyone thought Alex was a bit peculiar—everyone but Alex, that is. He knew exactly what he was doing.

Keeping distances in relationships was important for Alex. Early in life, he experienced the cruel fact that he couldn't trust anyone in his family. He realized that if he acted strangely in his birth home, people would leave him alone. In order to deal with the emotional and physical pain of his abusive father and neglectful mother, Alex decided to become the family "oddball."

It worked in his birth home. It worked at school. It kept his foster parents at a distance. It was a tactic that seven-year-old Alex perfected to avoid any attempts at closeness. It kept people and pain far away.

Just as in the stories of the other children mentioned above, Alex's adoptive parents understood him. They had a powerful ability to communicate love unconditionally — even to Alex in his most unlovable moments. Today at age ten, Alex still exhibits some behaviors that turn his peers away. But one of the happiest moments for his parents was the day he received his first invitation to a neighborhood birthday party. They saw in that little gesture from a friend that Alex was being accepted more readily. He was on the road to a more happy and healthy life.

These older children walk through the doors of adoptive homes each year. They can't articulate their pain, but their behavior does. As parents understand the coping mechanisms employed by their child, they will be better equipped to wade through the crusty exteriors to reach and help heal the broken-hearted child inside.

One adoptive mother recently commented:

My husband and I were talking the other day about the progress our five-year-old was making. We found ourselves asking, "Where would he be today if we hadn't been there?" We were greatly humbled by the thought and thankful that we had been given such a rewarding opportunity in a child's life.

SUMMARY

As parents prepare to begin adoption, they have several options that they might pursue:

- Public agency adoption — through direct adoption or foster care adoption
- Intercountry adoption
- Independent adoption

When children join their adoptive family, parents must take into consideration their children's inherited genetic temperament, talents, and abilities in forming their expectations. Parents must also be aware of the type of family situation their older adopted children came from and the role they may have assumed for survival. Those possible roles include:

- The competent child
- The withdrawn child
- The bully
- The manipulator
- The compliant child
- The peculiar child

QUESTIONS FOR SMALL GROUPS

1. What process of adoption is best suited for you? Why?

2. What difficulties have you encountered?

3. What type of children do you feel you could best parent?

4. Why isn't love enough?

CHAPTER THREE

What Builds Healthy Adoptive Families?

Ten Critical Success Factors

All children who need to be looked after outside their own homes,
for whatever reason, are children at risk. . . . The people who adopt them
are in a unique position to prevent life crises
from becoming pathogenic, to prevent separation experiences
from developing into deprivation,
to provide the kind of upbringing for each child
that will make good his past deficiencies.[1]
Sula Wolff, *Children Under Stress*

J on and Cheryl made a wise decision. Before the arrival of
their newly adopted infant twins, they sought the wisdom of
experienced adoptive couples. They knew that building an adoptive family was, in most ways, like parenting birth children, but
would require skills and knowledge beyond that of the ordinary
family.

At an adoptive parent support-group meeting, Jon and
Cheryl asked an important question: What goes into creating
a healthy adoptive family? This chapter will explore what they
learned that night.

SUCCESS FACTORS FOR HEALTHY ADOPTIVE FAMILIES

By incorporating ten critical factors into the parenting process,
adoptive families will be well on the way to a successful experience. To ignore them can rip away at the beauty and foundation
of this unique relationship of promise.

47

FACTOR ONE: PARENTS DEMONSTRATE HEALTHY FAMILY CHARACTERISTICS

Healthy family characteristics can be categorized in the following four areas.

1. *Parents model a strong marital relationship.* In his book *How's Your Family?* Dr. Jerry Lewis discusses areas that determine family competence. "Although many things go into the making of a healthy family," he says, "none is more important than the nature of the parents' relationship."[2]

Answers to a number of questions shed light on the health of the marriage: Who carries the power in the relationship? Is it equally shared with mutual respect? What are the levels of communication achieved in the family? Is there a sense of intimacy in the marriage? What is the quality and intensity of the marital alliance? How well do the individual personalities fit together?[3]

2. *Parents demonstrate the ability to resolve conflicts and problems.* Perhaps the most important function of the healthy home is the ability of family members to resolve conflicts. Individuals within a family develop their own style of conflict resolution. Some will yield to the other simply to avoid conflict. Some withdraw. Others deny there is a problem or dominate the weaker partner.

To the extent that parents rely on the process of negotiation, families confront and resolve problems in a positive way. Conflict resolution within the marriage rarely occurs in the birth families of children adopted at an older age.

3. *Family members evidence the ability to deal with feelings.* Adoptive parents who allow each other to express a range of feelings and respond empathically will create an atmosphere in which a child can do likewise. Families who block feelings or deny their existence will block the healing of those wounds that are deeply rooted in a child.

4. *Family members show the ability to accept and deal with change.* When a new child enters the family, either an infant or an older child, the entire family system shifts. New patterns of interaction and everyday living evolve. New relationships form. Stresses unique to this experience arise, and occasionally the adopted child bears the brunt of blame.

A healthy adoptive family understands that this kind of

change is temporary: The family shifting will eventually lessen and give way to a new normalcy. The family members persevere through the unsettled environment, all taking responsibility for working through the change.

FACTOR TWO: PARENTS ARE IN FULL AGREEMENT WITH THE ADOPTION

As the adoptive relationship begins and matures, one of three sets of interactive roles can develop between the parents: dynamic-dormant, active-antagonistic, or energetic-energetic. Either partner can play either role.

Dynamic-Dormant Parent Roles

Kathy waited for Robert to meet her at the adoptive training session. Although quiet by nature, Robert was abnormally uncommunicative about this adoption idea. Usually assertive with him, Kathy didn't want to push this issue. She just wanted to know where he stood. Whenever she asked him, his only response was, "If that's want you want." Kathy knew Robert wasn't against it. But she wondered, "Is he for it?"

Robert and Kathy Cook's *dynamic-dormant* parent style can be damaging to an adoptive placement. Nationally known adoption specialist Barbara Tremtiere calls this the "dragger and the draggee." The dynamic person in this family wholeheartedly pursues adoption. The dormant one hesitantly follows along, rarely expressing his or her thoughts.

A problem arising in this adoption triad (mom, dad, and child) is that once the child comes, the dormant partner tends to retreat from developing a parenting relationship with the newest family member. When conflicts arise, the dormant partner offers little consolation and marginal support, quietly reminding the dynamic one that the problems belong totally to him or her.

Active-Antagonistic Parent Roles

Patty nervously twisted a loose string on her jacket. She just wasn't sure how her husband, John, would "behave." He wasn't exactly enthusiastic about this whole adoption thing.

As they sat waiting in their car for the training room to open, the atmosphere was silent and tense. Patty, a warm and nurturing mother of two teenagers, missed caring for young children. She had long carried a dream to adopt.

John was an "all-business" type of father. He let Patty know that he wasn't very interested in doing this "child thing" all over again.

"I hope this doesn't last long," he complained.

"Don't worry," assured Patty. "I promise this will be my responsibility. You won't have to do a thing."

John and Patty Wyman definitely fit the active-antagonistic parent style. Adoptive parents within this disposition follow a basic line of thinking. One is for it; the other is against it. But they try to keep the tension a secret from others outside the family.

From the very beginning the antagonistic partner generally avoids contact with the agency. Nonessential issues become major. After the child arrives, the resistant partner avoids all situations that would allow him or her to develop a relationship with the child and often finds more excuses to be away from home. As the adoptive placement continues, the active spouse must learn to juggle the relationships of each person in the family in order to keep peace. Often that person becomes the dumping ground for frustrations from all sides and soon grows weary of the role.

Energetic-Energetic Parent Roles

Paul and Judy Walker arrived early and waited in the hall outside the training room. Adoption had originally been Paul's idea, but Judy enthusiastically agreed. This energetic-energetic parent style promises a strong foundation for beginning adoptive parenting. Both Paul and Judy are excited about it and have committed themselves to share equally in the parenting tasks.

Building a family through adoption can promote dynamic growth and understanding within the family. This has the best chance of happening in an environment of mutual support, common goals, and equal energy for the task.

Adjusting for Adoptive Parent Roles

When confronted with the assignment of assessing their adoptive parent styles, all three couples learned several concepts that helped them discern their individual roles and make adjustments accordingly.

1. *Explore the motivation for adoption.* Discuss if one partner seems passive or resistant to becoming an adoptive parent. Explore the reasons why. Those reasons may range from fear of the experience to questioning one's abilities to take on the task. It may not be the right time. This evaluation may require that the family reconsider and wait to begin.

2. *Keep in mind that attitudes toward adoption may fluctuate.* Circumstances can affect anyone's outlook on any given day. The long-term perception of the experience is what's crucial to the long-term commitment.

3. *Adjust expectations for each other.* One adoptive mom said, "I expected my husband to plan regular activities with our new son. When he didn't, I became frustrated with him. Expecting him to jump right in when he didn't know where he stood with Jimmy was unfair."

4. *Keep communication open and honest as the responsibilities increase.* Judy, a struggling first-time adoptive mother of two active toddlers, commented,

> I dreaded getting up in the morning and facing the tasks of the day. The honeymoon period with Katie and Callie had dimmed. I was exhausted, and I gradually grew resentful of them. But I kept my fatigue and anxieties hidden. Of course, it wasn't the girls. They were my absolute joy. I had neglected to communicate my own needs. That was the wrong approach. I just didn't want to appear to be a failure.

FACTOR THREE: PARENTS DISPLAY ACCEPTANCE OF THEIR OWN CONFLICTING EMOTIONS[4]

Families who adopt older children sometimes find themselves responding to their children in a manner that not only surprises them but also plunges them into guilt.

One adoptive mom remarked, "On some days, I have less patience, less tolerance. My discipline is harsher. What also surprises me is that I have felt such anger toward John one moment and such love the next."

For emotionally stable adults, it is unsettling to experience sudden surges of rage and unexpected changes in affection for a child. Children adopted during middle childhood may have conflicts and accompanying negative behaviors that frequently bring out these powerful feelings in adults. The adoptive parents, in turn, wrestle with feelings of guilt and shame because of their responses.

Adults can take a positive approach by realizing that these negative feelings are inevitable and refraining from so readily passing judgment on themselves for them. Linda Katz of Lutheran Social Services encourages parents to recognize that uncomfortable feelings will pass and that they can feel angry without acting it out and hurting the child. Expressing these feelings can diffuse reactive emotions and short-circuit the cycle of guilt, shame, and anger.

Healthy adoptive parents understand the need to maintain open communication regarding their own needs and struggles with each other and with those who understand the adoption experience.

FACTOR FOUR: PARENTS DEMONSTRATE THE ABILITY TO DEFER PARENTAL FULFILLMENT IN TERMS OF APPRECIATION AND ATTACHMENT AND REFUSE TO BE REJECTED BY THE CHILD

It takes a strong measure of persistence to parent a child who at the parent's most vulnerable moments cries, "You're not my real mother!" An adoptive parent of an infant may not experience that outcry until the youngster enters a crisis period in adolescence. Healthy parents understand adoption issues that create such an outburst.

Successful adoptive parents of children with prior birth home experience understand that instead of affectionate, satisfying responses from a child, they may receive anger and rage. These parents also understand that these behaviors are a protection against the fear of desperately needed closeness. They discern that the rejection aimed their way is triggered by past circumstances and really has nothing to do with them. And they have learned how to meet their child's needs in the home while postponing their own needs, sometimes for a very long time.

FACTOR FIVE: PARENTS ARE ABLE TO FIND SATISFACTION IN SMALL STEPS OF IMPROVEMENT

Adoptive parents often bring with them the preconceived notion of making or remaking a child into their dream. They place unreachable goals in front of the child and express dissatisfaction when those particular goals are not accomplished.

Healthy adoptive families focus not on long-range expectations but on achievable, short-term targets.

David was three months old when Robert and Kathy took him into their home. Their natural expectations were that he would mature normally, making it through each developmental stage with ease. They hadn't expected to parent a child who was markedly delayed in crucial areas. But instead of bemoaning David's difficulties, they took great delight in celebrating each new step of progress.

As David grew older, it also became apparent that school would be difficult for him. So this couple found something for David to do in which he could have a sense of success. David loved to collect rocks and shells. The family spent many happy Saturday afternoons at the lake, searching the shorelines with David for his treasured finds.

FACTOR SIX: PARENTS MAINTAIN A COMMITMENT TO THE PERMANENCY OF THE FAMILY RELATIONSHIP DURING DIFFICULT TIMES

Statistics vary, but a portion of older child adoptions (those occurring after the child reaches age three) dissolve by parental request when the child hits the unsettling adolescent years.

Infant adoptions are not immune to this dissolution, either. One particular therapist in Ohio who works with adoptive families in crisis mentioned that over two-thirds of her caseload involves parents and children who entered the adoptive experience years earlier, when the teen was an infant.

Why do parents who once promised to be that forever family sometimes waver over an impending decision to relinquish their vow? There are many grave factors involved in termination of adoptive parental rights.

One interesting perspective may pinpoint a partial reason

why adoptive parents back down from the greatest challenge of their lives. It has to do with the attitudes of adults today.

Parents during the eighties and nineties form a unique generation. They are called the "Baby Boomers," those people who were born between 1946 and 1964. In the process of development, Baby Boomers have redefined some basic life values. One of these is commitment.

Commitment takes a negative rap with today's parents of the Baby Boomer generation, according to researcher George Barna. They view commitment negatively "because it limits our ability to feel independent and free, to experience new things, to change our minds on the spur of the moment and to focus upon self-gratification rather than helping others."[5]

What does this belief have to do with adoptive parents? Some parents begin adoption with a dream of what it will be like. In fashioning their dream, they ignore realistic input. Not far into the journey, the dream begins to fade when reality is not what they expected. When the relationship stops feeling good, when the crises erupt, when tension and stress loom over the home, some parents question whether their relationship with their adopted child can continue.

Following this Baby Boomer approach to commitment, "people [some adoptive parents] willingly make commitments [to a child] only when the expected outcome exceeds what they must sacrifice as a result of that commitment."[6] Because adoption is based on a promise, and because promises can be affected by circumstances, the adoptive relationship is at risk.

Healthy adoptive families maintain their commitment to a child even when the reality is very difficult. If circumstances require professional services outside the home, they look for care options such as a residential treatment home. They close the back door. They work through problems as a family and do not permanently terminate the relationship with the adopted child. When the pain threatens the pleasure, they opt for hope, not out.

FACTOR SEVEN: PARENTS LIKE THEMSELVES

A primary characteristic of successful adoptive parents is personal self-esteem. The challenges of parenting, whether the child entered the family by birth or by adoption, can bombard parents with questions of self-doubt and failure.

As a child matures and asks more penetrating questions, a parent may deal with incredible feelings of rejection or being devalued as a person entitled to parent that child.

An older adopted child may discover that adoptive parents are the closest dumping grounds for a host of negative emotions.

Parents who consider themselves competent and capable will weather these storms successfully. They will allow the child to wade through those troubled times and find his or her adoptive parents waiting on the other side.

FACTOR EIGHT: PARENTS ARE OPEN TO SEEKING PROFESSIONAL HELP OR SUPPORT FROM OTHERS WHEN NECESSARY

A family's success with an emotionally needy child is often determined by their openness to disclose weakness and struggle within their own household.

The adoptive family, especially with an older child, requires a larger framework of assistance than does the family parenting birth children. This network of services includes social workers, school teachers, and therapists. Families who willingly acknowledge that their special task requires special assistance and who view that help as inclusive, not intrusive, will create a more healthy adoptive environment.

Jon and Mary, adoptive parents of two handicapped children, commented, "When it's the day for the speech therapist or physical therapist to come, we don't say, 'Oh no, those people are coming today.' They're our friends. When no one around us really understands what we are going through, they do. They are our support."

FACTOR NINE: PARENTS VALUE DIFFERENCES

Each child who is adopted arrives with a bushel full of differences from his adoptive family. The most obvious, of course, may be physical appearance. As the child grows, differences will emerge in mannerisms, interests, habits, and performance ability.

Successful adoptive families value these differences rather than rejecting them. They highlight the positive distinctions that create the child's unique individuality. They put in respectful focus the various dissimilarities that set the child apart from his or her adoptive family.

FACTOR TEN: PARENTS BUILD THEIR FAMILIES WITH A STRONG VALUES STRUCTURE

Healthy parents build their family environment with values based on personal convictions that are respected and communicated. They also understand that the wisdom, strength, determination, and encouragement needed for all of life come from beyond themselves.

"Of all the odd times and places to gain some insight into our situation," Janice related, "it was the day I was on my hands and knees scrubbing out the bathroom tub." She went on to explain:

> Justin was twelve when he came into our home as a foster child. At thirteen, his birth parents' parental rights were terminated, so adoption was a natural thing for us to consider. My husband had a terrific relationship with him. I could not get beyond a civil and sometimes uncivil response most of the time. I wanted so much to feel love for this child and for him to reciprocate. I felt guilty and angry most of the time for my feelings toward him and the situation.
>
> One afternoon, as I was down on my hands and knees cleaning the bathroom, I asked God for wisdom and insight into our situation. I simply asked why my relationship with Justin wasn't working. Immediately, some things I had been told in parenting classes a few years earlier about older children came to mind. The answers came so keenly that I stopped what I was doing and wrote them down.

Here are the insights Janice gained that day:

> First, I was expecting Justin to love me as a mother. But he had had no positive female figures in his life. To him, a woman meant rejection. He wasn't capable of trusting me at that point in his life.
>
> Second, this boy had never had the opportunity to

deal with the issues of his past. He was stuck in emotional quicksand, struggling to free himself but afraid of what would happen when he did.

Third, Justin was nearing a time in his life as an adolescent when independence was a primary task. I was trying to pull him in to attachment, at a time in his life when he was grasping for wings.

The list continued. That day, as I reflected on the insights freshly learned, I released my anger and frustration. I felt for the first time I could freely share my problems with Justin with friends, not fearing the judgmental looks that I had failed. Most important, I had a strong sense that God was gently leading, strengthening, and empowering us for this particular challenge in our lives. We were not alone.

Families who choose to adopt face parenting demands unknown to parents raising their birth children. "You've got to be optimistic without denying what is happening," advises child advocate Susan Edelstein. "You've got to focus on strengths, keep perspective, set reasonable goals and get help when you need it. You have to be able to tolerate the unknown. You have to be able to say, 'I will love this child forever.'"[7]

SUMMARY

Healthy adoptive families recognize factors of success that can guide them through the experience. These factors are:

- Parents demonstrate healthy family characteristics.
- Parents are in full agreement with the adoption.
- Parents display acceptance of their own conflicting emotions.
- Parents demonstrate the ability to defer parental fulfillment in terms of appreciation and attachment and refuse to be rejected by the child.
- Parents are able to find satisfaction in small steps of improvement.

- Parents maintain a commitment to the permanency of the family relationship during difficult times.
- Parents like themselves.
- Parents are open to seeking professional help or support from others when necessary.
- Parents value differences.
- Parents build their families with a strong values structure, based on personal convictions that are respected and communicated. They also understand that the wisdom, strength, determination, and encouragement needed for all of life comes from beyond themselves.

QUESTIONS FOR SMALL GROUPS

1. What other traits of successful adoptive parents have you observed?

2. Of the factors mentioned in this chapter, what do you feel are your strengths? What do you feel are your weaknesses?

3. How do you feel about the "Baby Boomer" attitude toward commitment? In what ways, if any, do you think that this attitude affects the adoption experience?

4. If you have made a "promise" to the child you adopted, has it been tested? How have you handled the stress and ambivalence?

CHAPTER FOUR

Developing a Supportive Adoption Environment:

How to Prepare Biological Children, Family, and Friends

Natural child: any child who is not artificial.
Real parent: any parent who is not imaginary.
Your own child: any child who is not someone else's child.
Adopted child: a natural child, with a real parent, who is all my own.[1]
Rita Law

Cathy Fraley hung up the phone, disgusted with herself again. Whenever she mentioned adoption to her parents, there was always a conflict. They just didn't seem to understand the dream she and Daniel shared. Her parents didn't want them to adopt, particularly not an older child.

"It's too shaky," they said. "What if it doesn't work?" The last words Cathy's mother said to her that day were, "I don't know if I can love that other child like I do your sons."

Adoptive parents such as Cathy and Daniel discover with the first step into the journey that their decision affects many lives and activates many responses. They know that adoption involves more people than just a child and the parents, but they're often unaware of how extensive an environment is affected in some way by their decision.

Within that environment are the other children in the family, members of both extended families, and a circle of influence made up of friends, neighbors, church, and school. All parties touched by the adoption have reactions that will influence the family's adoption experience, either positively or negatively.

Usually, the unsettling responses result from a lack of knowledge and understanding. However, as adoptive families recognize the needs of their birth children, educate their extended family members, and learn to manage responses from within their circle of influence, they will find the foundation of their "promise" strengthened by family and community support.

BLENDING FAMILY MEMBERS TOGETHER – WALKING A TIGHTROPE

Blending family relationships of birth and adopted children can be like attempting to walk a tightrope high above a circus ring. Leaning too far to the right or left can send the acrobat tumbling off. This challenge holds equal priority with establishing adoptive parent-child relationships.

Adoptive families report that their difficulties in this challenge range from conflicts over space and possessions to extreme sibling rivalry, anger, and aggression.

The birth child already in the home can encounter problems in developing a relationship with the new sibling or in coping with all the changes brought about by the addition of this newest member.

One major reason why birth children experience stress is that familiar roles no longer work well and new roles must be acquired.[2] In addition to learning these new roles, biological children must master new unwritten rules, grasp how to communicate about the newest family member, and cope with ambivalent feelings that are new to them.

"DOESN'T MOM LOVE ME ANYMORE?" – BALANCING AFFECTION AND ATTENTION

Eight-year-old Rick sat on the back porch looking dejected. His father slipped in beside him on the picnic bench.

"What's wrong, son?" Rob asked.

Rick's eyes filled with tears. "Does Mom still love me?" he asked softly. "She just doesn't act the same since Jason and Sally came here. Doesn't she love me anymore?"

Rob, Shelley, and Rick are a close family unit. All three of them made a decision to add to their family through adoption because they felt that their family could offer love and security to other children. However, it seemed to Rick that things changed quickly. One afternoon, he was an only child. The next afternoon, he had a new ten-year-old brother and a new three-year-old sister.

When the Rizers said yes to these two children, they stepped out onto a tightrope. They had to learn to meet the needs of the household's newest members without neglecting their birth son. Shelley commented:

> When the children first came, I tried to make everything equal for them. If I hugged one child, I hugged all three. The problem was that Jason and Sally didn't want much of that. In the midst of their uneasiness, I tried to act the same way toward all three of them. I wanted to love them just the way I loved Rick. I felt guilty because it wasn't happening. In a effort to balance everything, I found myself withdrawing some of my affection from our birth son, so the other two wouldn't feel slighted.

Rick's evening conversation with his father opened their eyes to what was happening inside their shifting family system. Rob and Shelley took specific steps that relieved the pressure felt by all family members.

First, to deal with the issue of equal attention for all, Shelley and Rob realized that they could love the children not *equally*, but *distinctively*. The Rizers had to become students of their new family members. They watched the children together. They talked with Jason about his birth family relationships. They inquired more fully of caseworkers, former foster parents, and others who knew the children and the environment of their birth home. They adjusted their own expectations and needs of responsiveness from the children. They discerned that a progression of attachment needed to occur, not an instantaneous one.

Shelley and Rob also adapted three principles that helped

them deal with the balancing act.

1. *Instead of giving equal quantities* ("Here, now you have as many cherries as your brother"), *they gave according to individual need* ("Do you want a few cherries or a big bunch?").

2. *Instead of attempting to balance actions of love* ("I love you children all the same"), *they showed each child that he or she was loved uniquely* ("You were born with special gifts and talents: there is no one else in this world like you").

3. *Instead of attempting to balance equal time* ("I will go to everyone's game every week this year"), *they scheduled according to need* ("What activity of yours is important for me to attend this week?").[3]

By modeling healthy relationships over the three years that Jason and Sally have been part of the family, this sensitive couple has led all three of their children into the style of closeness enjoyed in their home. Grimaced resistance has given way to spontaneous hugs. The boys relate together and enjoy teasing their little sister, who is learning to handle "obnoxious" older brothers appropriately.

"WHY DIDN'T HE GET IN TROUBLE?" — BALANCING PRIVILEGES AND DISCIPLINE

Seven-year-old Steven, birth son of Denny and Sue Benton, stormed into the family room.

"Kevin said he didn't get into ANY trouble for what happened at school today. It's not fair! If I did that, I'd have to stay in my room all evening."

One particular challenge that tests parenting skills and patience to the limit in any home is the issue of equal privileges and equal discipline. In a family where birth and adopted children grow up together, the pressures can be even more intense.

The conflicts were erupting early in the adjustment period for the Benton household, who had added nine-year-old Kevin to the family just three months earlier. Sue described their challenge:

It's so hard to decide what's fair when meting out privileges or discipline. In some ways our birth son is more mature and responsible, although he is two years younger. Sometimes we must allow him an opportunity that Kevin is not yet ready for due to his immaturity. On the other hand, Steven has certain academic standards that he must maintain. Kevin is not required to meet those same standards. Therefore, Steven may experience some discipline in areas where Kevin is allowed more space.

As Steven turned to leave the family room, Denny stopped him. "Son, it's time for us to talk. Let's go for a walk." During that time together, Denny described more about Kevin's background to Steven. He explained the reasons for how they were handling school problems and other situations as well. Most importantly, Denny attempted to identify with Steven's feelings and frustrations, not criticize him for them.

The simple activity of giving Steven more information and tuning in to his feelings provided him with a broader understanding. The result was that it greatly reduced the hostility between the two new brothers.

"SHE'S NOT YOUR REAL SISTER" —
LEARNING TO HANDLE COMMENTS AND QUESTIONS
FROM THE NEIGHBORHOOD KIDS

When three-month-old Jennifer joined the Smith family, seven-year-old Karen was excited. She couldn't wait to walk down the street to the playground and tell her friends all about her new baby sister. But she wasn't prepared for the questions and comments from curious youngsters. "Who is she? What do you mean, she's adopted? Where are her real parents?"

Karen went home that afternoon and told her parents what had happened. Although they had taken considerable time to explain the meaning of adoption to Karen, they realized they had not equipped her to deal with her neighborhood friends. Don and Sylvia helped their young birth daughter by giving her a story to share when she was asked about the adoption. The story grew out of a few straightforward "handles" Karen could hold on to when talking about her new sister:

1. A simple, factual explanation of how Jennifer came to live

with the family.

2. The understanding that adoption is a different way to join a family—not more desirable or less desirable, just different.

3. Terminology that would present adoption in a positive, realistic way. Terms such as "she joined our family," not "she was put up for adoption," and "birth mother," not "real mom," assisted Karen in sharing with her friends.

"WHY DID SHE HAVE TO COME HERE ANYWAY?" — COPING WITH FEELINGS OF JEALOUSY AND RESENTMENT

Of the biological children in the home, the one who struggles the most with acceptance is usually the one displaced in birth order by the newest family member.[4] A child who had been the oldest or youngest may now be the middle child. A girl who enjoyed her role as the only one of several boys in a family may suddenly find herself displaced by a new sister.

The results can be anger, resentment, and a surprising change in attitude and behavior. Even teenagers, such as Donna Burch, now nineteen, struggle with adjustment.

Donna was sixteen when their family made a joint decision to adopt two girls, ages nine and ten. Her mother and father enjoyed the parenting role and, like many adoptive parents in the middle years of life, decided to do it again. Donna recalled:

> I figured I would be going to college soon and really wouldn't be around. But the agency contacted us much sooner than I thought they would, and the girls moved in. One day I had my own bedroom, my own bathroom, my own makeup, and my own clothes. Then all of a sudden there were three of us.
>
> Going from the only child left at home and the baby of the family to being a big sister was a bigger challenge for me than I thought it would be. I didn't know what to do with the girls at first. It was hard to learn what to say, how to act, and how to feel about them. I was surprised that sometimes I reacted badly toward them because I couldn't talk with my parents without curious ears around. I felt that I had lost my space.

The most important response by Donna's parents during this adjustment period was not to lecture her on her "negative behavior." In the early stages of adjustment, they did not try to force Donna's attitude to change by expectations that were unreasonable. They did not say, "You should do better than this," or, "You have had so much more than these children, you should be thankful."

Instead, Donna's parents allowed her the room she needed to work through her feelings. They asked her opinion about how they should handle things with the girls, affirmed their love and her place in the family, and expressed their confidence that Donna would make the right choices.

Heather and Holly have since been invading Donna's "space" for over three years. As time progressed Donna's parents did challenge her to consider the two choices she had. One choice was to become bitter and resentful because of the time that was taken away from her relationship with her parents. The second choice was to invest something of herself in both girls. Donna made the second choice. She says of the experience:

> It has made me a different person. It's the best thing
> that ever happened to our family. I would probably be
> extremely self-centered as a young adult if I had not had
> the opportunity to see how some other kids have had to
> live. I know that now at nineteen, I appreciate my own
> family more. I am much more sensitive to the needs of
> children who were deprived of the love that I was fortunate
> to have.

Donna's plans for the future include pursuing a degree in social work—specifically, the adoption field.

After adoptive parents, the children born into the family are next in line in terms of handling adjustments when a new child enters the home. If parents address their birth children's displacement issues, such as loss of attention, demand for equal discipline, and feelings of lost position and space, they will help smooth the transition.

HOW TO GAIN SUPPORT FROM THE EXTENDED FAMILY

Dear Jack and Bonnie,

I feel I must write a few lines to make sure that you don't misunderstand our feelings concerning your adoption of the twins. I want you to know that we share in your joy, if it is for the best. I feel a real strain right now. I am afraid that you don't understand our concern. Do you think we are against you and that we can't talk things over?

This is a very big step you are taking right now — so much adjustment with two babies at one time. No doubt you can learn not to buy material things that you don't need so you will have enough money for a family of five. But what about the possible strain of adjustment with different dispositions involved? Also, what about your marriage and the strain it will feel?

We just pray for the best. Please don't forget that we love you. If you adopt these young children, they will be loved equally as our grandchildren.

Love,

Mom Wallace

When a couple first thinks about adopting either an infant or an older child, there are two sets of special people whose responses hold great influence — their own parents. The approval or disapproval of parents and other extended family members is often used as a compass for couples as they determine the direction they will go.

Generally, extended family members hesitate in giving their full approval to a couple's dreams because of three major areas of concern. With the help of the agency or other support persons, couples can usually alleviate these apprehensions by offering further explanations to their family. Most often, enthusiastic support follows.

COMMUNICATING THE DECISION TO ADOPT

For a young couple dealing with infertility issues, the question of why they are adopting is quickly answered. Obviously, they still have a desire to raise a family.

For families who choose to adopt older children, a child of a different race, or a sibling group, the question can be more penetrating.

Here are two ways to communicate an adoption decision more effectively.

1. *Introduce the idea as a tentative plan.* If the family has no hint that you have been considering this decision, don't present it as a finalized goal.

It took the Coles ten hours to drive to Oklahoma for a visit with Tim's parents. Every once and a while, Tim kept reminding Kathy, "Don't say anything about our plans to adopt from Korea. Let me handle it my way. I know Mom and Dad."

The first night at the dinner table, Kathy kept dropping hints to Tim to tell them the news. As the dessert was being passed, Kathy could wait no longer.

"Guess what we are going to do?" she asked. "We are going to adopt a two-year-old from Korea."

Tim's parents looked at each other and then directly at Tim. After a moment's silence, his father simply inquired, "How are you planning to pay for it?"

The rest of that vacation week was spent in near silence on all sides. Tim's parents, who had previously no clue to their plans, felt totally left out of a very important decision. Because Kathy ignored Tim's request for handling the timing carefully, the young couple returned home without the initial and essential support of his parents.

2. *Develop creative ways to educate family members.* David and Jody shared their initial plans with both sets of parents. Because they were new to the whole process themselves, they couldn't answer some of the questions and concerns family members raised. They decided to do something unusual. They invited their agency adoption worker and two other prospective adoptive families and their parents to a casual informational meeting.

During the meeting, the worker told the families how the process of adoption worked, what to expect from the child, and how to prepare for the arrival. Following that meeting, both sets of prospective grandparents joined their children in anticipating the new child. The education session about the entire adoption program eased many of their apprehensions.

WHERE DO WE FIT IN?

One of the uncertainties that can block a grandparent from embracing the idea of adoption is their place in the child's life. Establishing this new relationship with an infant or toddler is not as threatening to grandparents as building an attachment with an older child or a youngster from a different race or culture.

Before their adopted son Daniel arrived, David and Jody Miller talked with the grandparents to be. They reassured them that they didn't expect "love at first sight" for either party, Daniel or the grandparents. Sure, it *might* happen, but more than likely it would take time.

Jody and David communicated to their relatives that building a family connection with an older child is a process that grows with "love actions," such as positive affirming conversation, kindness, and sensitivity.

The Millers also suggested that their parents could do the following things to help bridge the gap:

1. Take pictures of the new child and display them with those of other family members. It would help them to redefine the family unit.[5]

2. Join the Millers in celebrating adoption day. Encourage all family members to establish this anniversary as part of family rituals such as birthdays and holidays.

3. Establish a new tradition that is special just for the grandparents and the new child—for example, taking initiative to be the one who teaches the youngster to fish or to develop a new hobby or sport. This kind of tradition will long be remembered.

4. Choose the names the child will use for his or her grandparents. David and Jody did not assume that they knew what their parents wanted to be called. Choosing a special name for first-time grandparents of an adopted child would be treated the same way as choosing a name for grandparents of a genetically related grandchild.

Daniel was the first grandchild in the family, on both sides. It was a special honor for both sets of grandparents to come up with the name by which Daniel and the other grandchildren to follow would call them. When they met the four-year-old, they were introduced by those special names.

WILL YOU BE DEPRIVING THE OTHER CHILDREN IN THE HOME?

Although most adopters' parents fully support the adoption before as well as after, there is almost always a complete swing to full approval once the child joins the household.[6] For families with birth children already present, however, the initial support from grandparents is substantially less until the family integrates the new member. Grandparents tend to be very protective of their grandchildren.

When Ron and Charlene Williams decided to adopt, one of the first reactions of both their families was, "What about Robbie? Won't he be deprived? Won't these children take away time from you that belongs to him?"

The Williams were prepared for their parents' concerns. They discussed their considerations with them, legitimizing instead of diminishing them. They reassured their parents that they were keenly aware of their need to balance the new relationships in the home without neglecting Robbie.

Ron and Charlene's openness on these issues helped alleviate their parents' anxieties. After five years, the relationship between grandparents and their new grandchildren is energized by a deep love and acceptance. All the children hold equal importance. When this couple decided to adopt again, their parents asked the same question, only with a different slant: "What about Robbie, Patrick, and Lynne? Won't they be deprived? Won't this child take away time from you that belongs to them?"

As adoptive parents consider the adoptive environment of their extended family, they can prepare by making a promise to each other: to forgive any insensitive, callous remark or action made by a family member. Long-term grudges will only weaken the whole family system.

It is important to grasp a significant concept that relates to potential responses from family members. Grandparents may value the "blood ties" more than ties created by adoption. The relationship of promise creates a different connection for them as well. Their different response is not intentional or planned. It is covert, possibly subconscious, yet it emerges through comments and behavior, as occurred in this incident:

> One woman, the oldest of three daughters, reminisced that her adopted son was the first grandchild for the parents. To all appearances, they were very pleased with the child. But when one of her younger sisters . . . became pregnant, the baby crib which had been in the family for several generations, and in which the three girls had also slept, was given to the couple expecting this baby.[7]

The prospective grandparents never thought of offering the crib to the adoptive family. This kind of behavior can cause resentment in couples who are desperately attempting to place equal dignity and position on their role as adoptive parents.

Covert sentiments also surface during family interaction surrounding holidays and birthdays. Adoptive parents should encourage relatives to be sensitive about giving gifts. Attempts at building adoptive grandparent relationships with an older youngster can be thwarted if a child perceives that he or she is valued as secondhand. Simple communication about this issue can head off potential problems.

ADOPTION WITHIN THE COMMUNITY— UNDERSTANDING PERCEPTIONS

One final group of people makes up the adoptive environment: the family's circle of influence in schools, churches, and neighborhoods. Adoptive parents often find that individuals in their local community view adoptive parenting differently than rearing a birth child. Even well-intentioned comments that are made without thinking can alienate members of the adoptive family from those very people whose support they need.

"What a nice thing for you to do, adopting that biracial child."

"What do you know about her background?"

"How well you care for your baby boy—just like a real

mother!"

"Maybe the reason he doesn't do well in school is because he's adopted."

Adoptive families can successfully manage the outside world that affects them and their children by taking five positive steps.

First, just as Don and Sylvia did for their daughter, *parents can develop and use a vocabulary of positive language for discussing adoption* (see table 4.1).

Table 4.1: Positive Language for Discussing Adoption[8]

POSITIVE TERMINOLOGY	NEGATIVE TERMINOLOGY
Birth parent (father, mother)	Real parents
Adoption triad (birth parents, adopted child/adult, and adoptive parents)	Adoption triangle (implies conflict)
Made an adoption plan	Adopted out, given away Unwanted child
Child joined the family	Child was put up for adoption
Child came to us through adoption	Child was surrendered Child was abandoned
Their birth children	Their own children (when excluding the adopted child)
Their children	Their real children
My child	My adopted child
The waiting child	Hard-to-place child
Special/medical needs child	Handicapped/difficult child
Search, reunion	Track down his real parents

Second, *parents should make it a practice not to disclose private information about the child to anyone outside the trusted immediate family.*[9] Once information is given out, both the adoptive parents and the adopted child have lost any control over who knows it and whether it will be misunderstood or misused later at the wrong time or in the wrong way.

Third, as with comments from family members, *parents should not hold a grudge because of thoughtless statements.* One adoptive father said, "We simply made the choice not to let it bother us. If we responded emotionally to every inconsiderate or unthinking remark, we would be exhausted."

Fourth, *educate those with whom the child has regular contact,* such as school teachers or Sunday school staff. Ask them to consider the child carefully when making assignments that have to do with families of origin. Usually at least once in the grade school experience, a youngster is asked to bring baby and family pictures. Children who were older when adopted are unlikely to have such photos.

Finally, *ask professionals who regularly encounter the child to inform you as the parents if the child appears to be having any emotional difficulties.* During the middle school years, children experience a sense of loss regarding their genetic ties. Dr. David Brodzinsky, a psychologist, found that some youngsters in these middle years appear to have more psychological and school-related behavior problems and more difficulty getting along with their peers than do their non-adopted peers.[10] However, even though these youngsters have more problems, the majority of them are well adjusted and their difficulties do not require professional services.

QUESTIONS THAT DESERVE A RESPONSE

Adoptive parents are frequently inundated with questions not only from household members but also from extended family, friends, colleagues, and acquaintances.

The two questions that come up most often are "Why adopt?"—especially when the child is seriously ill, retarded, biracial, or advanced in age—and "What makes this child adoptable?" These questions deserve a response from a spiritual perspective.[11]

To answer the first question—"Why would you accept someone else's child as your own?"—adoptive parents can look to a higher principle in life.

This principle, at the heart of how and why hundreds of adoptive families guide their lives, can be called *voluntary redemptive suffering.*[12]

Wrapping one's heartstrings around someone else's child is a *voluntary* choice. Each year, hundreds upon hundreds of adoptive parents around this nation voluntarily stand before a judge to make a promise to a stranger's child: "We will be your family, forever, by our choice to do so."

Adoption is not only voluntary; it is also *redemptive*. "Redeem" means to release, to make up for, to restore. An adoptive family's guiding light is the vision to restore to an abused or neglected child the dignity of life that was ripped from him. It is a dignity that child was born to enjoy.

In addition to being voluntary and redemptive, adoption involves *suffering*.

To extend your energies around the clock with no guarantee of a night's rest to care for a seriously ill child—that is suffering.

To be told, "You're not my real mom/dad," and to continue to give love in spite of that rejection—that is suffering.

To see a child recoil from affection because of years of abuse, and to know that you would gladly carry the pain for them but can't—that is suffering.

Why do people adopt? Because they live their lives by a spiritual principle—*voluntary redemptive suffering*.

To answer the second question—"What makes a child adoptable?"—adoptive parents can again focus on a higher principle: *the value of life itself*.

In an age that values life only if it is productive and its presence convenient, there are still adoptive families who see beyond the ugly consequences of severe abuse, beyond the fears of debilitating handicaps, beyond the barriers of age or race. They look beyond all these things and see a child. They see a life that by virtue of its very existence has worth, value, and promise. They see a child in need of adoption.

Yes, families still volunteer to take the risks inherent in restoring dignity to a child. In the process, they willingly suffer disappointment and pain. Yet they still choose to adopt because of their strong belief in the value of life. As they reach out to the abused, neglected, and dejected, these families are piloted by the Giver of life himself.

SUMMARY

When a couple decides to adopt, they must not only prepare themselves but equip those in the adoptive environment. These individuals include the biological children in the home, extended family members, and neighbors, friends, and professionals in their circle of influence.

Issues for the birth child include:

1. Balancing affection and attention
2. Balancing privileges and discipline
3. Learning how to communicate about the new child
4. Coping with feelings of jealousy and resentment

Issues for extended family members include:

1. Gaining their support
2. Communicating the decision to adopt
3. Helping them understand where they fit in
4. The question of depriving other children in the home

Issues for friends, neighbors, and professionals in the local community include:

1. Developing and using a vocabulary of positive language for discussing adoption
2. Disclosing information selectively
3. Managing and forgiving unthinking or insensitive remarks
4. Educating professionals and others with whom the child has regular contact

---

QUESTIONS FOR SMALL GROUPS

1. What kinds of comments have you received from family, friends, and acquaintances regarding your decision to adopt?

2. Has anyone made insensitive remarks to you or your child? How did you handle them?

3. What suggestions do you have for dealing with others' curiosity, particularly concerning a transracial adoption?

4. What difficulties have you encountered with the children who are already a part of your family? How have you dealt with these difficulties?

5. What have you told school or church professionals regarding your child? How much do you feel they should know?

PART TWO

When
a Child
Comes
Home

CHAPTER FIVE

Attachment:

How to Develop the Crucial Bond

*One of the most difficult things for adoptive parents to accept is the fact
that nothing can change their adopted child's genes,
early life experiences, or ties to another family. . . . Only by allowing
a child this heritage from the birth family,
and incorporating it into the current family,
can that child really belong to the adoptive family.*
Bourguignon

B enjamin had experienced more trauma by age two than many
adults go through in their whole lifetime. He had survived
incredible, life-threatening starvation. His mother, who was born
in India, had abandoned him, and he had lived in multiple orphan-
ages. His life was immersed in filth and poverty — not only environmental poverty, but emotional and psychological impoverishment.

At two-and-a-half, Benjamin was handed to his American
adoptive parents at the Detroit airport by a stranger whose only
contact with him was caring for him on a long-distance flight.

Upon arrival, Benje exhibited behaviors typical of children
with attachment distress or disorder. He became rigid when his
parents attempted to cuddle him. He would not make eye contact
with them.

Just like Benje, hundreds of children (from U.S. adoptions as
well as overseas) enter their adoptive homes exhibiting behaviors
that are foreign to their new families. For parents who adopt
infants, it is important to understand the process of attachment

in those early crucial months. For parents adopting children who have experienced more than one significant caregiver in their early life, it is critical to understand how the dynamics of attachment can affect their relationship with the child in the initial stages of adjustment and beyond.

As parents understand the significance of attachment and recognize symptoms of attachment distress or disorders, they can create a positive, accepting environment for their newest family member.

BUILDING ATTACHMENTS IN THE ADOPTIVE HOME

Jennifer slumped onto the couch, exhausted. It was her husband's turn to walk the baby. Their new son, two-month-old Jonathan, had been in their home for only one week. Arriving from Honduras, he had not adjusted to any schedule. His days and nights were confused and all he would do was cry.

"I really don't think I am cut out to be a mother," Jennifer remarked to Jodie, another adoptive mom who had stopped in for a visit. "I feel so frustrated and angry with this child."

Jodie got up, walked over to the couch, and sat down next to Jennifer.

"I know it's difficult," Jodie empathized. "I've been there. He is still a stranger who won't let you rest, isn't he? You haven't fallen in love with him yet."

Jennifer looked at Jodie with an incredible sense of relief. Torn with guilt, frazzled by exhaustion, Ted and Jennifer felt anything but love for this child. Worst of all, they felt like complete failures. They didn't realize that a very important process was taking place, but it was only in its infancy. That process was attachment—the deep sense of belonging to each other.

WHY IS ATTACHMENT SO IMPORTANT?

Attachment has been defined as the psychological connection between people that permits them to have significance to one another.[1]

Attachment, according to psychologist Jean-Pierre Bourguignon, is a learned behavior that begins shortly after birth and continues during the first three years of life. Attachment occurs over time and involves a consistent activity on the part of the parent to meet the physical and emotional needs of the child. The capacity to form new attachments after the age of three is quite possible, but is affected by three factors: the child's own genetic disposition, the conditions and circumstances under which the child is taught, and the child's teachers.[2]

Attachment is the foundational core of any intimate relationship. Secure, early attachments create a rich treasury of important life functions. Attachment enables the child to develop a sense of safety and security. Eventually, it gives rise to other crucial functions such as socialization, stimulation of intellectual development, and identity formation, according to Vera Falhberg, pediatrician and specialist in the field of adoption attachments. Dr. Falhberg also cites other long-range effects of attachments:[3]

1. Helps a child to sort out perceptions of the world in which he lives
2. Encourages the development of logical thinking
3. Develops social emotions in a child
4. Cultivates the formation of a conscience
5. Helps an individual cope with stress, frustration, worries, and fears
6. Fashions an appropriate balance between dependence and independence
7. Sets the stage for the unfolding of healthy future relationships

HOW DOES ATTACHMENT OCCUR?

Attachment is reciprocal in nature as the relationship between parent and child grows. It develops as the infant initiates a need and the parents respond. As the child's physical and emotional needs are consistently met by the same caregiver (usually parents), the child learns that he or she is safe, secure, and can trust this responsive person. Attachment is created through the consistency of the caregiver's response to the child's needs and the child's reception of these positive messages.

ATTACHMENT RESPONSES IN ADOPTED INFANTS
Children adopted as infants display little difference in their quality of attachment from non-adopted infants, reports Dr. David Brodzinsky, noted psychologist and author. Adopted mother-infant pairs tend to look almost exactly like biological pairs. Differences don't show up until infants are past the age of six months.[4]

A psychiatrist at the University of California at Irvine, Dr. Justin McCall studied the adjustment behaviors of infants moving to an adoptive home. McCall noted that in the first six months of life, distress manifests itself in greater or lesser degrees as eating and/or sleeping difficulties, spitting up, chronic diarrhea, and crying for no reason. Extreme cases can result in the development of failure to thrive—a psychological condition in which an infant loses the will to live.[5]

McCall's continuing observations of infants past the age of six months show that these children have developed a more advanced way of signaling distress, including: "searching behaviors as though looking for his caretaker; uncontrollable crying, withdrawal, uninterested in playing or eating, clinging behavior, lack of vitality, frequent weight loss or illness."[6]

Even though some infants do manifest such behavioral difficulties, Dr. Brodzinsky notes that children are generally incredibly resilient. "In fact," he comments, "the evidence suggests that the great majority of these children adjust quite normally."[7]

AS THE CHILD GROWS

INFANT ATTACHMENT: A CRUCIAL LIFE NEED
Ted and Jennifer fortunately learned early that building attachments with their precious new son was a process. It involved many of the following behaviors:

1. Enjoying physical contact with the infant: holding, rubbing, cuddling, stroking, kissing.
2. Developing face-to-face contact, particularly emphasizing eye contact.
3. Responding and repeating a child's vocalizations and verbal expressions.

4. Using a gentle tone of voice.
5. Learning appropriate age-development skills for the child and working with the youngster in mastering them.
6. Looking for and identifying characteristics of the child that remind them of themselves or extended family members.[8]

How can adoptive parents know that their efforts to create attachment between themselves and their infant are succeeding? According to specialists in this area, a measure of successful attachment can be monitored by the parents' sensitivity to the child's need signals, their initiation in responding to those signals, their confidence in meeting the child's needs, and the child's responsiveness to them. Another prime indicator of strong attachment is the child's positive response upon returning to the parents following a brief separation.

If adoptive parents recognize symptoms of attachment distress or deficit in their infant or toddler, professional guidance may be required. Therapists who specialize in such difficulties work with the child and the parents in establishing this essential emotional and psychological need.

OLDER CHILD ATTACHMENTS: REBUILDING BROKEN PIECES

A hard fact of life for families adopting older children is that interruptions in attachments do cause harm and pain for a child. For these children, rebuilding attachments requires sensitivity, openness, and knowledge of what children need.

Positive parenting practices (see following box) will aid adoptive parents in rebuilding the sense of attachment in their child. The importance of early intervention is extremely critical.

POSITIVE PARENTING PRACTICES[9]

■ Parents show enthusiastic interest in child's development and autonomy. They work on building the child's self-concept by supporting skill-building efforts and emotional closeness.

- Parents express a healthy and informed interest in meeting all of the child's environmental needs, including personal preferences in clothing, food, and room decoration. Also, parents direct the child in learning proper hygiene and dental care, and respond quickly to an illness.

- The adoptive parents' priorities are balanced so that frequent time is spent with the child, especially a young child. Activities are shared and the communication is positive. Non-parental child care should be warm, consistent, and adequately supervised.

- The parents allow the child to try tasks independently in order to gain self-awareness and confidence. Parents do not overprotect the child from experiencing normal life stress, including the normal cycle of frustration, persistence, and self-accomplishment.

- The parents' response to the child is warm, loving, and nurturing, with an ability to comfort the child in a positive way. Laughter and joy are frequently expressed in the home.

- Discipline is balanced with love, logic, fairness, and consistency. Chores are designed to promote responsibility, pride, and self-respect.

- Parents support the child's intellectual, emotional, spiritual, and social growth by attending school functions, helping with homework, and encouraging healthy peer and extended family relationships.

In addition to incorporating these normal attaching behaviors into healthy family living, several other suggestions for dealing with the attachment issues and loss resolution of an older child are provided by Linda Bayless:[10]

1. View the child's behavior as an opportunity to re-parent. As mentioned earlier, the child will most likely regress in skills already mastered (for example, bed wetting or school problems). As the regression occurs, parents can take the opportunity to interact with the child in a positive, reassuring manner.
2. Identify something each parent can do with the child for a short period of time every day. The activity can be as short as fifteen minutes, but should be pleasurable to both participants. If the youngster is resistant to such involvement, back off the effort temporarily. Work toward shorter segments of time doing something together.
3. Immediately incorporate the child into "nonsignificant" family traditions, such as whose turn it is to sit by Dad at the dinner table or who gets the front seat.
4. Depending on the child's age, give him or her a responsibility to fulfill as part of the family.
5. Allow the child to have mementos and memories of significant people. If the child is older, having some contact with those significant people (such as former foster parents) may be important.
6. Parents can share with the child memories of their own past losses and the ways in which those were resolved.
7. Ask children to identify familiar and special things in their past that are important to them. Recognizing such things as how they celebrated holidays and favorite meals or activities communicates to children that *all* their life is important to the family, not just their life since joining the adoptive family.

DISTINCTIVE BEHAVIORS OF CHILDREN WITH ATTACHMENT DISTRESS

Children who suffer with attachment deficits have lost the ability to trust those people and relationships in their environment. They have long forgotten the feelings that accompany security and safety. They don't know what it's like to have a consistent adult in their life who meets their basic needs.

Children who demonstrate the lack of attachment may fall into one of three categories, according to Bourguignon:[11]

1. The *non-attached child* never attached to a parent or primary caregiver in his early life experiences. He never knew the meaning of safety, security, and trust given to him by those responsible for his care.

2. The *inadequately attached child* is typically found in the foster care system or possibly as a result of the moves involved in an international adoption. This child's primary attachments were disrupted, sporadic, or extremely unhealthy. He has bounced from one caregiver to another.

3. The *traumatized child* had the opportunity to form a primary attachment and receive crucial nurturing in his early years. However, in the course of growing up, this child experienced a severe trauma such as sexual abuse, physical abuse, or emotional neglect. The results destroyed the early trust built within the child.

As a result of difficult circumstances prior to adoption, these children may enter their adoptive home exhibiting behaviors indicative of attachment disorders. The following sections describe some of these behaviors and suggest how parents can cope with them.[12]

Withdrawal and Rejecting Behavior
Rejection creates deep, long-lasting wounds in the heart of its recipient. It destroys a child's sense of worth and damages his ability to function in life with confidence. It directs its victim to remained detached from potentially significant people in his world to avoid pain. In some youngsters, withdrawal is anger turned inward.

How can parents cope? Parents can best rebuild the shattered heart of the withdrawn child by developing consistent ways to express love. Positive, constant reinforcement of the child's sense of value and worth, with assurance that the child's worth is not based on performance, will eventually fill the empty places. (See chapter 9 for a thorough discussion of particular things parents can do to accomplish this reinforcement.)

Adoptive parents must also realize that they will more than

likely have to continue their efforts to greater or lesser degrees into the adulthood of their child, because a rejected spirit leaves a person vulnerable and fragile to new relationships.

For Ken, an adoptive father, one of the happiest parts of his day was coming home after work, because he looked forward to seeing his wife and three children. But coming home after work was also one of the hardest parts of his day, because Ken had to face Eric, his newly adopted three-year-old son. He longed for Eric to run into his arms. But Eric didn't come near him. In fact, Eric acted as if his new father wasn't even there. Ken felt terribly rejected and terribly disappointed. What had he done to deserve such treatment from a toddler?

Eric's rejecting behavior of Ken is typical of a newly placed child who has experienced rejection and separation from his birth family or another significant caregiver. In Eric's case, his only memories of his abusive birth father were that he was violent and unpredictable. In his young, subconscious mind, he had determined not to allow himself to have any relationship with a father figure.

After talking with another adoptive father who had experienced the same relational disappointment, Ken was relieved. He learned that Eric was not rejecting him personally, only what Ken represented. Ken was encouraged by his friend to continue to reach out to Eric in small, positive steps and to make sure any discipline was well-balanced with positive interaction and play. He was also directed to avoid putting any time expectations upon Eric and their relationship.

Because of what Ken learned, he was able to relax and quit worrying. He took small, positive steps to nurture Eric, beginning by joining his wife, Sarah, in putting Eric to bed. Eventually, he conducted the evening ritual totally by himself. Sarah also took more opportunities to allow Ken to baby-sit. Leaving Eric with Ken alone for an hour soon built up to a whole Saturday afternoon.

Several months later, almost without notice, Eric warmed up to Ken. Soon, one of the happiest times of Ken's day was coming home from work each day to find Eric sitting on his tricycle next to the mailbox, waiting for him.

Hoarding or Gorging Food

For the third time in one day, Marcia found a loaf of bread, a box of crackers, and cookies in Aaron's toy box. She quietly took Aaron to his room and pointed out what she had found. She gently reassured him that it was not necessary to hide food in his room. Anything he needed would be available upon request.

Aaron's behavior is typical of children adopted from Third World nations, where the incredible fear of never knowing where the next meal will come from is an everyday fact of life. This behavior also emerges in children from this country who suffered serious deprivation, emotionally as well as physically.

Kate, the adoptive mom of three-year-old Lucy, explained that her daughter will often communicate in her own little way, "If you love me, you will feed me." For this child, food and love amount to the same thing.

"The closest these children can come to feeling loved is eating sugar," one authority commented. "They get that exhilaration — sort of being loved."[13]

Dr. Kenneth Magid points out that these children have "chronic emptiness inside":

> They have emotional wants that need to be sated. Some
> may try to fill this emptiness with food and this often
> can take the form of stealing and hoarding food. . . . This
> emptiness doesn't mean that the child was deprived of
> food as an infant, although it can. Often the hoarding or
> gorging is an unconscious reflex brought on by the terrible,
> unexplained empty feeling inside.[14]

How can parents cope? For a family dealing with this particular problem, it is an encouragement to know that this behavior will dissipate. It is a good idea not to overreact to it, or to use food as a tool of correction or a sign of affection. This particular child needs a great deal of emotional reassurance demonstrated through physical interaction — kisses, hugs, playful wrestling. It could take as long as a year for the child to settle into his new home and feel comfortable enough that food is no longer an attachment issue.

Aggressive Behavior

Whether a child is one or five, when entering an adoptive home he can react to his life experiences of abuse, neglect, or abandonment with rage. Aggression against those in his new world or against himself may be his only tool for releasing pent-up feelings that he can't communicate.

As a response to fear, frustration, or anger, some children display aggressive behavior. The older they are, the more opportunity they have had to learn that this aggression keeps people at a distance. They don't have to face their fears and distrust of the adults in their world. They take out their feelings either on people in their world, their physical environment, or themselves.

At age two, Karie was moved into her third home. Bounced from relative to relative and eventually into foster care, she was an angry, aggressive toddler. She inflicted pain upon herself, literally ripping out her hair by the handful. She would also bite herself until her arm bled.

How can parents cope? The number-one perspective for parents dealing with an aggressive child is *time*. It takes a great deal of time for changes in this kind of behavior pattern to occur. Parents will deal with this reality more effectively by breaking down needed changes into smaller increments.

In Karie's case, her parents didn't delay in contacting a therapist to help them learn ways to direct Karie's angry outbursts. They gave her a stuffed animal, encouraging her to vent her frustrations on it. After a period of time, she was able to do that.

Today Karie has grown into a well-adjusted, happy six-year-old with long, lovely hair. She is delightful to be with and a joy to her parents. Although she still has occasional bouts with tantrums, she has learned more appropriate ways of handling them. Like Karie, even very young children respond to play therapy and can overcome uncontrolled outbursts. Karie's adoptive parents also made clear to her that she was allowed a reasonable mode of expressing herself in the house.

Physically aggressive children deal with low self-worth. They believe that they are never good enough. Physical affection is important for these children, even though they may initially reject it.

Lying and Stealing

Adoptive parents of older children are often frustrated by deceptive behaviors in their child. For many children, lying and stealing have developed as a way to survive the chaotic home environment: "Lying is a self-protective device and a way to avoid
punishment and embarrassment. Some children do it more out of
habit and fear than anger or necessity. The concepts of 'truth' and
personal ownership may hold little meaning for children who
have been promised so much and had so little. Conscience development may be quite delayed."[15]

Some unattached children, says Dr. Magid, lie all the time, not
just once in a while. They lie even when it doesn't seem to have
any purpose, such as what they ate for lunch or who they played
with at school. Dr. Foster Cline, a nationally recognized specialist
on attachment, comments that "it is almost as if the child confuses
the way he *wishes* life were with the way it *actually* is."[16]

How can parents cope? With children who lie and steal, parents should avoid harsh, unrealistic physical punishment but be
firm and consistent, allowing the child to face either natural consequences or disciplinary consequences. If a child steals from
a store, he should return the stolen object to the manager and
face whatever action the store imposes. If he lies to a teacher, he
should face the normal consequences dictated by school rules.

Natural consequences register deeply in the minds of youngsters. They may be painful for parents to watch, but they are the
most important character rebuilding instrument available. For
some of these children, facing consequence after consequence is
the only hope for a future free from this disabling habit.

Often these children have no idea why they lie; they just
do. To help them recognize what they did, parents can create an
accepting environment in which children learn that it is safe and
right to tell the truth. Consistent confrontation of these children,
pointing out their deceptive behavior and asking them to describe
it as well, allows children to hear and acknowledge verbally what
they have done. They should also be asked to verbalize the consequences of their behavior.

Again, working regularly with a counselor or therapist who
specializes in this type of problem is a high priority.

Poor Eye Contact

A child who mistrusts his world may demonstrate an inability to make eye contact. Uncertain of a response from an abusive parent, a youngster has learned to avoid such intimacy.

According to Dr. Magid, unattached children will not look their new parents in the eye. "The only time they do have good eye contacts is when they are extremely angry, or want something and are being very manipulative."[17]

How can parents cope? One primary task of a new adoptive parent is to work at establishing eye contact. If the child is an infant or still needs to be fed, this time provides a good opportunity to have the child look at the one who is feeding him.

One mother began using a technique that was suggested to her at an adoptive parents support group: place her infant daughter's bottle to her mouth and tip it for feeding only after her baby had established eye contact with her (without, of course, postponing feeding too long). This method finally succeeded after five to seven months, and the infant began responding at the correct developmental level for her age.[18]

(Lois Melina, author of *Raising Adopted Children*, points out that in some cultures, direct eye contact is considered a gesture of disrespect. In cases where this cultural background is a factor, lack of eye contact may not indicate lack of attachment.)

Delayed Conscience Development

Children with a delayed conscience display little or no emotion when confronted with misbehavior. They have developed a survival system of lies and fantasy, in which they do not have to assume any responsibility. These youngsters become masters of manipulation.

How can parents cope? This type of attachment disorder is a difficult one for parents to address. It requires the assistance of professionals who can guide the parents according to the child's and family's individual and collective needs.

Indiscriminate Affection

A child with a lack of attachment will be driven by overwhelming need to pursue and find affection and attention even from strangers. At age three, Taylor has lived with four different families since leaving his birth home. He freely sits on the lap of anyone who will allow him to, whether he knows that person or not. For Taylor, there are no "strangers."

How can parents cope? Children who do not discriminate between strangers and more intimate relationships have had no internalized person identified as "mother" or "father." One important step a parent can take, therefore, is to avoid multiple caregivers.

If both parents must work outside the home, they should avoid daycare centers and hire a baby-sitter who can be the sole non-parental caregiver consistently.

All adopted children have experienced the breaking of crucial bonds that lead to emotional, intellectual, psychological, and physical health. However, as parents recognize their children's attachment needs, they will do a much better job of working through the adjustment stages.

SUMMARY

Attachment to a significant person is one of the most important achievements for an infant, because it creates a rich treasury of positive life functions such as a sense of security and safety and skills for socialization. Healthy attachments also stimulate intellectual development and identity formation.

Attachment occurs as a child initiates a need and the parents consistently respond. The child eventually learns that he can trust his environment.

Children who never had the opportunity to form an attachment, due to circumstances in their birth home or surrounding their separation from their birth mother, may exhibit some of the following behavioral symptoms:

- Withdrawal and rejecting behavior
- Hoarding or gorging food
- Aggressive behavior
- Lying and stealing
- Poor eye contact

■ Delayed conscience development
■ Indiscriminate affection

These behavioral signs may indicate that a child is in desperate need of attaching to a significant person—a parent. Studies have shown that as a child attaches, many of these behaviors will diminish or even disappear.

QUESTIONS FOR SMALL GROUPS
1. What behaviors have you experienced that are similar to those mentioned in this chapter?
2. How have you dealt with these behaviors with your child?
3. How did those behaviors affect you and your family?

CHAPTER SIX

Barriers to Adjustment:
Strategies to Ease the Transition

Adoptive parents who bridge the adjustment barriers understand two things.
First, their child has had a tremendous loss — loss of both parents,
genealogical ties, cultural heritage, to cite a few.
Second, that child may emotionally revisit those losses at crossroads
on their journey through childhood into young adulthood.
Family Ties

Jerry was home from work that afternoon when the call came from the adoption agency. As anticipated, a teenage birth mother had decided on adoption for her newborn son. Would they be interested in discussing the child further? Could they come that evening?

Jerry and Carol Smith had waited three years for this moment. Life without a child and the long days and weeks of roller-coaster waiting might finally be coming to an end. "Yes, we'll be there this evening," Jerry answered.

Sharon Ryan hung up the phone. She could hardly contain herself. The adoption social worker had just called, asking Sharon and David to come in the next day and discuss the possible adoptive placement of two siblings, a four-year-old boy and a one-year-old girl.

Neither Sharon nor David slept well that night. Tomorrow they would face a decision that would affect them and two very special youngsters for the rest of their lives.

Every day in this country, prospective adoptive families receive such a phone call. It is an emotionally charged moment, and it creates an atmosphere of intense anticipation and anxiety. Questions flood their minds as they begin to wrestle with such a monumental consideration.

"Is this the right child? How can I prepare for him? Will we be good parents? Can we *truly* love a child born to another person? What if our parents won't accept this child?"

There are two primary ways that couples can prepare themselves for the moment when a child moves in with them. First, they can learn as much about the child as possible from the agency and other involved persons. Second, in the case of children who arrive through the foster care system or international networks, they can learn to recognize the potential adjustment barriers that may affect the initial relationship with a child who is older when joining his or her family.

This chapter will present an overview of the initial barriers to adjustment with suggestions for how to cope. (Chapter 9 will discuss how to build a nurturing environment that responds to the attachment needs, behavioral adjustments, and long-term issues of all adopted children at whatever age they entered the home.)

HOW MUCH CAN I KNOW ABOUT MY CHILD?

Jerry and Carol sat in one conference room at the agency; David and Sharon sat in another. Both families held pictures in their hands. For the Smiths, it was a beautiful picture of a three-day-old boy, with eyes open and alert. For the Ryans, it was a picture of two beautiful children, Matthew and Katie.

Tears welled up in Sharon's eyes. She had dreamed of this moment for years. Hope had almost faded that it would ever come. Gwen, the Ryans' adoptive social worker, interrupted their thoughts.

"Mr. and Mrs. Ryan, what questions do you have concerning the children?" she asked. "This is an important time for you prior to making the decision whether to pursue adoption of these children. We want you to have as much knowledge as possible so that you can make a balanced, objective decision."

David pulled from his pocket a long list of questions they had prepared well in advance of this occasion. Faced with a dilemma that no biological parents ever consider, this young couple had to decide whether to take on the responsibility of parenting children not born to them.

Throughout the course of the two-hour discussion, the Ryans asked the following questions. Many of these same questions can be pursued by parents adopting an infant or adopting overseas. However, regrettably, in many cases of overseas adoption this information is unavailable, not collected, or not shared.

1. Why were the children removed from their biological family?
2. What social and medical history is available on the father? On the mother? On the grandparents?
3. Is there a history of drug or alcohol abuse?
4. What was the children's home environment like?
5. What is their history of abuse? Of sexual abuse? Of neglect?
6. When was their last contact with their biological family?
7. Have Matthew and Katie been prepared in any way for this move? What have they been told?
8. How did they cope in foster care?
9. How many moves have they encountered? Why?
10. How have each of them responded to those moves?
11. Are there any other brothers and sisters?
12. What contact have Matthew and Katie had with siblings? Is it expected that this contact will continue, and to what degree? Who is responsible for seeing that it happens?
13. Who was the primary caregiver to the children prior to removal from their family of origin? Who was the primary abuser?
14. What is known about the children's birth history?
15. What is known about the children's developmental history — physically, mentally, and emotionally?

16. Is there any evidence of mental or physical handicaps?
17. What is their current health? Are there any problems, such as allergies? Are they current with shots and checkups?
18. What particular behavioral difficulties do they appear to demonstrate? Tantrums, soiling, bed wetting, aggression, withdrawal?
19. What methods of discipline work well with Matthew and with Katie?
20. How does Matthew relate to his peers at preschool?
21. How do the children respond to change?
22. If Matthew and Katie have been in therapy and/or in a foster home, what steps will be taken to meet with these individuals?

The Ryans concluded their initial interview with Gwen feeling that they had received a tremendous amount of information about the children. Although they strongly sensed that these children would be a welcome addition to their home, they asked Gwen to give them a week to consider their decision. David and Sharon recognized the importance of not rushing such a decision in this fragile moment. They didn't want their emotions to dictate such a critical step.

BARRIERS TO COMING HOME

Matthew opened the back door and ran through the living room, bubbling with excitement.

"Did Mommy Janet call yet?" he shouted.

"No, Matt," Sharon replied. "She hasn't. But the minute she does, I will call you to the phone."

Mommy Janet was Matt's foster mother. He and eventually his younger sister had lived in her home before moving in with the Ryans. Although he had been in their home for over three months, he still talked a lot about Janet. This made Sharon feel discouraged. She wanted to be his mom, but for now she had to share the role.

When the parent-child relationship begins there are several dynamics happening within the child or adoptive couple that may present a barrier to a smooth adjustment. Acknowledging and attending to these barriers can minimize their impact and smooth the transition for all family members.

FROM THE CHILD'S PERSPECTIVE

BARRIER ONE — UNFINISHED BUSINESS:
DEALING WITH SEPARATION AND LOSS[1]

Matthew had experienced the loss of significant relationships in his young life. First, he experienced the loss of his primary, vital connection when he was taken from his birth mother at age two as a result of physical abuse. Then he moved into his foster home and reestablished an attachment to a primary important person, only to face a second separation. His ties to his foster mother had been incredibly strong.

When Matthew joined the Ryans at age four, he was not emotionally ready to transfer his maternal attachment needs to yet a new mother. He was still in the stages of grieving his most recent loss.

Children (and toddlers) who experience circumstances like Matthew's usually progress through several stages in early reactions to loss. Adoption expert Claudi Jewett Jarrett (author of *Helping Children Cope with Separation and Loss*), along with other specialists in the field, outlines these stages within two general phases: early grief and acute grief.

First Phase: Early Grief

1. *Shock and numbing.* When initially told of an impending separation or loss, children may respond with little emotion. This is numbness: the sense that it is not really happening to them and must be happening to someone else.

2. *Alarm.* There is a physical reaction to the shock of separation, according to Jarrett. These reactions may manifest themselves in a rise in heart rate, muscular tension, sweating, dry mouth, bowel and bladder relaxation, and even shortness of breath. Insomnia has also been noted as a response to loss. Additionally, children appear to be susceptible to infection when undergoing the tremendous stress of loss and change. It is not

unusual for a child to suffer with a respiratory infection or gas-
trointestinal disturbance.

3. *Denial and disbelief.* Children in this stage of grieving
appear to reject the reality of the situation completely. Annie,
age six, moved into her adoptive home without ever having the
opportunity to say goodbye to her birth father. For a brief period
of time she would run into the house explaining, "My daddy just
drove down the street. He still wants to see me."

Because her father lived in another state, Annie's sightings
were impossible. They appeared to be part of her denial and disbelief that her relationship with her father was really over.

Second Phase: Acute Grief

1. *Yearning and pining.* This stage in the grieving process is common to all who experience a significant loss. Matthew was at this
point as he coped with the separations of his life. Deep inside
he longed for the restoration of his relationship with his foster
mother, yet at the same time he felt the conflict of a budding
attachment to Sharon, his new adoptive mother.

According to Jarrett, "regression is a common companion to
the conflict and fatigue that results from the yearning and pining
stage."[2] It had been years since Matthew wanted to be rocked to
sleep, but now he demanded such attention at bedtime. Long
past the usual bed-wetting stage, Sharon found herself changing
bedding almost daily.

Some children may step back in time, shelving a developmental skill they mastered earlier in favor of returning to behavior from an earlier period in their lives.

Adoptive parents who recognize such behavior in their child
can be encouraged with the knowledge that this regression is
only temporary. Children whose parents allow them to retreat
to former territory will eventually establish a new perspective.

2. *Searching and bargaining.* A form of magical thinking can
develop in a person who suffers the trauma of loss. Often,
children may consciously or unconsciously make a "bargain."
They may promise always to be good. They may promise never
to love anyone else.

A step away from yearning, this stage contains several

elements, according to Jarrett.[3]

One aspect of this stage is marked by children being absorbed in and passionate about the lost person. They often display a compulsive need to talk about this, dwelling on past memories. They will refuse to talk of the present and its realities.

A second element of the searching and bargaining stage of acute grief emerges in children who demonstrate a sense of expecting something to happen. They may comment that the lost person might attend events they will be attending or might appear at places common to the child.

A third element is restless or somewhat hyperactive behavior. The child may be unable to sit still or to focus for a period of time on tasks placed before him. Occasionally a child may be suspected of having behavioral problems when in reality he is working through tremendous grief issues.

Perhaps one of the most important assignments for adoptive parents caring for children at this point in their lives is to be patient in allowing children the expressions of grief that will appear.

Some adoptive parents report a sense of rejection by the child in this stage. They comment that their own coping mechanism was to cut the child off in the midst of his expressions of grief by reminding him that those things belong in the past. Jarrett suggests that "curt remarks urging the child not to dwell on the past only cut off the sharing and make the bereaved child feel misunderstood."[4]

3. *Strong feelings: anger, guilt, and shame.* The Barretts had been told to expect Lorrie's outbursts of strong feelings. And sure enough, they soon broke the surface. "I hate you! I hate you!" Lorrie yelled at her adoptive mom. "Why did you ever have to come into my life?"

Facing this onslaught of anger without pulling away from a hurting child will demand strength, wisdom, and empathy from the adoptive parents. It is impossible to predict the length of such a stage, but specialists say that it may take as long as six to twelve weeks for the worst of the pain to subside.

4. *Despair.* This stage can be most disconcerting to parents,

who must watch their small child slip into a sense of hopelessness and helplessness. Although depressed children are not able to disclose any further what they are thinking or feeling, they will demonstrate behavioral changes such as extreme fatigue or changes in eating and sleeping habits.

Usually, this period in the grieving stage for children is not lengthy. As children move through it, they enter the final stage. For adoptive parents willing to walk on this painful, uncertain road, the following suggestions provide support.

First, *allow the child to express his feelings of sadness, anger, or grief* without relegating them to the past or negating their importance. Grief that is shoved under the rug will have to be uncovered later on.

Second, *keep the home schedule relatively free of constant activity*. Adoptive parents often attempt to help their children forget about the past by filling up their children's schedule. However, constant motion is not what these children need. Rather, they need an environment in which time for sharing and talking together is a priority.

Third, *remember the importance of physical touch*. Researchers say that people need eight to ten meaningful contacts a day to maintain emotional and physical health. Children feel strength from a parent who sits close to them when they are sharing strong feelings. A touch on a shoulder or a lap to sit in reassures a troubled youngster of secure love and concern.

As a child makes his way through these initial months of grieving, he eventually reaches the final stage of grief.

5. *Reorganization*. Parents of children who are moving into the stage of reorganization notice a brighter countenance and a better frame of mind. Teachers report improved behavior and grades. For the most part, neighborhood conflicts disappear.

After walking through the difficult stages of separation and loss, these children have now reorganized their lives without the missing adult at the core.

BARRIER TWO: LACK OF PREPARATION[5]
Selecting a child to fit into an adoptive family requires especially sensitive preparation if the youngster has formed a significant

attachment to another adult. If age permits, clear explanations should be given to the child of what is happening to him and when it's going to happen. If he is old enough, he should feel a sense of contribution to the decision. Any child who is forced to move quickly may become shell-shocked and confused.

Most successful placements of children begin with a pre-placement time that is used by all parties involved as a period of preparation.

Tom and Terri Adams answered enthusiastically to the prospect of six-month-old Paul joining their family. Their desire was to rush over to the foster home where he was living and bring him home that night. However, wisdom and sensitivity guided them.

During the first week, Tom and Terri began visiting Paul in the foster home, often staying two hours or more. Within that week, they took Paul on short trips and eventually on overnight visits. By the end of two full weeks, they were no longer strangers to this delightful youngster. He moved in with no major traumas to overcome.

Tom, Terri, and Paul's adjustment to each other was greatly eased because they did not rush through getting to know each other.

For children who are verbal, pre-placement visits provide them with space to integrate into their thinking what is happening in their world and to begin dealing with the changes and losses they will encounter.

A significant barrier to adjustment is erected when children are forced to make a move into a new family with little information about the process or the family they are joining. Even very young children observe, understand, and absorb more than what they are usually given credit for. Many adoptive families prepare a welcome book that is used by agency staff to introduce the child to the family before meeting them in person.

BARRIER THREE: CULTURAL DIFFERENCES
Susan was becoming increasingly worried about her new three-month-old, Korean-born daughter, Kim. Kim cried every time Susan put her down to accomplish some work around the house. Susan wasn't getting anything done. More importantly, she won-

dered if something was wrong with the baby.

A short time later, Susan learned at an adoptive parents group that Korean mothers carry their infants on their back while they work. Kim's problem was that she wanted the closeness she was used to sensing. Susan thought she would give it a try. She learned how to wrap the child on her back. It was awkward at first, but she soon realized that she enjoyed the closeness. Best of all, Kim stopped crying.

This young mother discovered that even infants may require some significant adjustments. Families who adopt from a foreign country should make the following inquiries to discover what kinds of adjustments may be necessary:

- What type of formula and food was the child given and in what manner? What type of eater (heavy, light, picky) was the child?
- When the baby fussed, what methods were used to console him?
- Where and how did the child sleep?
- Did the child demand attention, or was she content alone?

For parents adopting older children, the following suggestions may be helpful in making the transition:

- Be ready for some communication difficulties. If there is a person in the community who speaks the language of the child, ask permission to solicit help in times of distress, even in the late hours of the evening.
- Accept the child's non-Americanized mannerisms and lifestyle. Eventually the child will adopt American ways. It is not necessary to push him.
- Be aware of talking down to a child. Often when children are struggling with the language barrier, parents may treat them as far younger than their age. Or they speak very loudly, as though the child cannot hear well.
- Learn some significant customs from the child's country. For example, some countries celebrate birthdays

differently than the United States. This kind of celebration would be an excellent place to start.[6]

When children enter a new family, they face unforeseen barriers to adjustment. The same is true for their parents.

FROM THE PARENT'S PERSPECTIVE

BARRIER ONE — UNMET NEEDS AND UNMATCHED EXPECTATIONS

Sitting across from a counselor, Holly and Jeff had nothing left to say. In the midst of the pain attached to the crumbling of their adoption dream, they couldn't believe what they had just said.

Only a year ago, they had worked hard to prepare for five-year-old Joey coming to live with them. Today, torn with frustration caused by their perception of Joey's inability to blend into the family, they felt like giving up. They had had enough.

What had brought them to this crossroads? The answer lies in how Holly and Jeff began this journey. Two dynamics that are crucial to setting the course for building a relationship had been neglected:

- In the beginning, no one addressed this couple's needs for the relationship.
- In the beginning, no one addressed this couple's expectations for the experience.

Adoptive parents should consider their own needs during the process of deciding to parent a child born to someone else, because those needs will significantly affect the entire process. They will dictate a parent's response to adjustment issues.

What are these needs? Here are some that adoptive parents have voiced:

- "I have a strong maternal/paternal need to nurture a child."
- "I have a need for this child to see me as the only mother figure in the world. I need for him to forget his birth mother."

- "I have a need for this experience to be exactly the same as parenting a child born to me, since I can't have children of my own."
- "I have a need to feel a deep attachment to this child and she to me."
- "I have a need to give family membership to a needy child and to be appreciated for doing so."

And the list continues.

As they walk through the early months, adoptive parents must not only identify their own needs for the relationship but also examine their own expectations.

Occasionally, such parents create in their minds an image of the child they hope to adopt. They enter the relationship with high expectations of performance and behavior. When those expectations go unmet, they find it difficult to invest in the child.

Unmatched expectations regarding the child and others involved in the adoptive environment often create unyielding tension on the newly formed family system. The ground underneath the promise begins to shift.

What are some of those expectations? Again, here is what adoptive parents have said:

- "I expected my new child to appreciate all that I do for her. After all, look where she came from."
- "I expected my birth children to sacrifice for this new child in our home."
- "I expected my extended family to take to this new child as they would a birth child."
- "I expected the agency to be readily available to me with answers and support."
- "I expected that I would always feel happy and fulfilled because we've helped this child."

To greater or lesser degrees, many of these expectations are usually met. However, parents who are unable to adjust their expectations of the child, and of their birth children, their extended family, and the agency, will find themselves cornered in a maze of frustration without resources for finding their way out.

BARRIER TWO—MARITAL PROBLEMS

A significant ingredient for a smooth adjustment in the new family centers on the health of the marriage, as was mentioned in an earlier chapter.

In hopes of fixing a troubled marriage, some couples feel that the addition of a child will be the determining factor. Instead of relieving a stressful situation, however, it only compounds it.

Occasionally, other couples in a more stable marital situation enter into the adoptive relationship without being fully committed to it as a team. Because they are not in agreement, crises or stresses precipitated by the adoption often cause marital difficulties.

BARRIER THREE—REORDERED FAMILY SYSTEM

When a new family member enters the home, whether by birth or by adoption, the entire family system shifts. A comfortable equilibrium disappears, replaced by momentary confusion and relational chaos. How families respond to the shift will greatly determine how smoothly everyone walks through the adjustment phase of adoption.

One primary task new adoptive families must accept is to create a new management system. Within that management system are new household routines such as getting more children out the door to school, packing more lunches, cleaning more rooms, and running more errands. Also part of that management system are new rules, often unwritten, such as how much time is allotted for TV, free play, study, and work. Setting up the new family system can be a physically and emotionally exhausting endeavor.

Steve and Darlene Miller adopted one-year-old twins, Bradley and Jonathan. Steve described the shock of change:

> We didn't realize how we would react to the loss of privacy and freedom we encountered when the boys first

came. We were pretty much used to having time to ourselves and going when and where we pleased. We knew in our minds that those things would change. We didn't realize what it was like to live it. We were surprised that we would react in frustration to the change.

As soon as we perceived what was happening, we knew what to do about it. Instead of totally submerging ourselves in the children, we learned to balance time for them and for ourselves. We made plans for time together on a regular basis so that we could strengthen our own relationship, and didn't feel guilty about it.

BARRIER FOUR—INCOMPLETE RESOLUTION OF LOSS WITHIN THE PARENTS' OWN LIVES

Six years ago, Byron and Rachel Jones lost their only birth child to Sudden Infant Death Syndrome. Recovering from this tremendous loss continued to be a difficult process for them. Two years ago, they adopted an infant, bringing her to their home straight from the hospital.

Following that adoption, Byron and Rachel moved from the community where they had lived to new jobs and new friends. They told no one of their loss. They told no one of Kayla's adoption. They had made an unconscious decision to block out that pain from their past. Kayla was their daughter, and that was the way it was.

This young couple is not likely to face adjustment difficulties with Kayla in their early years together. She is a happy, energetic two-year-old. The difficulties will emerge later, when Kayla is eventually told of her adoption and Byron and Rachel must respond to her questions. Both parties in this adoption entered the relationship from the position of loss. Byron and Rachel lost a child. Kayla's losses include birth family ties and relationships. As adoptive parents, Byron and Rachel will become the interpreters of Kayla's losses, but more than likely will pursue them from the vantage point of how they handled their own—denial.

Adoptive parents assume many roles in the life of their child. However, none is as crucial as the role of becoming their child's "interpreter of loss."

For parents who adopt older children (either nationally or internationally), their role begins immediately as they provide a stable environment where a child feels her way through a potentially emotionally traumatizing period of her life.

For parents who adopt infants, in the years to follow the role of interpreter will eventually emerge and require an even greater depth of understanding. Such understanding most often comes as an outgrowth of an adult's own response to losses in his or her life.

What kinds of losses are we talking about? Adoptive parents face not only those normal losses that occur through life's transitions such as the death of a parent, loss of a job, or loss of a spouse, but also the losses that are unique to their particular life circumstances. As mentioned earlier, some of those losses include:

- Loss of a birth child, either by death or infertility
- Loss of dreams for family as planned
- Loss of status as birth parent
- Loss of providing grandparents with birth child

In order for adoptive parents to create an environment where children can deal with their losses, parents must know how to resolve their own. In *Faces of Rage*, author David Damico says that if we fail to resolve loss in a healthy manner it will have the following consequences:[7]

- We will impair our ability to recognize and comfort our children when they are in pain.
- We will injure our ability to feel and remember as our practice of blocking out bad times extends to difficulty in remembering good times as well.
- We will force ourselves into self-protection that will keep others at arm's length. For adoptive parents, lack of resolution will keep at arm's length any discussion that forces the family to confront the pain of loss in the child's life.
- We will project our own fears and beliefs into the pres-

ent circumstance. We will mistrust our child's motive
for wanting information about the past.

■ We will construct walls of rage that lock the needy
parts of ourselves inside away from anyone—including
God—who can heal and restore us. Adoptive parents
who have not walked through the pain that leads
to healing may lead their children in constructing
those same walls—which keep out pain but also block
healthy responses to loss.

Unresolved loss, warns Damico, "extends to every aspect of
our physical, emotional, and spiritual being."[8]

What are the ways in which adoptive parents face their
unique losses? Just as adopted children deal with loss by denying, bargaining, getting stuck in yearning or pining, or experiencing feelings of anger, rage, sadness, and despair, so do adoptive parents. In dealing with loss, these parents should work with
supportive friends or a counselor in identifying their loss, their
feelings about it, and the stage in which they find themselves.
Groups such as Resolve, which focuses on infertility issues, Com-
passionate Friends, which centers on dealing with the death of
a child, or adoptive parents support groups provide validation
for parents as they walk through those issues unique to their
circumstances.

Damico offers an encouraging insight into the subject of loss
resolution:

> When we allow ourselves to experience pain, hope begins
> to enter. It reminds us of the loss, which always hurts.
> But the reminder of loss helps us clear a path through
> the pain to a new shore. When we get there, we will be
> different—so will our world. Hope helps brings us to
> acceptance. Never ignoring or erasing loss or pain, hope
> teaches us to respect and honor loss. It brings dignity to
> pain. It makes us strong, more authentic and more under-
> standing of others whose losses mirror our own.[9]

And so will it be for our children.

SUMMARY

Preparing for a child to come into the home requires two steps by adoptive parents: (1) Learn as much about the child's past history and family as possible; (2) recognize the potential barriers that may slow the adjustment of the adoptive relationship for all family members. These barriers include:

- From the child: unfinished business, separation and loss, lack of preparation, and cultural differences.
- From the parents: unmet needs and unmatched expectations, marital problems, reordered family system, and incomplete resolution of loss in their own lives.

QUESTIONS FOR SMALL GROUPS

1. What other questions can be helpful in learning about a child?

2. How assertive can and should adoptive parents be in getting this information?

3. What other barriers to adjustment have you experienced?

4. How did you resolve these barriers?

PART THREE

Communicating About Adoption

CHAPTER SEVEN

How Do We Feel About Adoption?

Critical Questions for Parents and Children

I couldn't talk to my parents about adoption — I didn't want to hurt them.
I couldn't talk to my friends — they didn't know.
I keep that part of my life put away.
I grew up feeling isolated, alone, and different.
Sarah, age twenty-five

K ellie, age nine, called for her mother to come to her room. "Mom, I've been wondering. Why did my birth mother get rid of me?"

Beth wasn't prepared for this abrupt question. She and her husband, Jake, had always maintained open lines of communication with Kellie about her adoption. They shared with Kellie about the circumstances of how she came to live with them at the age of only two weeks. They repeatedly told her that not only had they gained a beautiful daughter, but she had acquired a family who deeply loved her.

Kellie had always seemed happy with that explanation — until now. What had happened?

Children like Kellie, who are adopted in infancy, obviously form their primary attachments to the adoptive family. Their emerging comprehension of what adoption means grows slowly with each passing cognitive developmental stage. An adopted child may begin to ask penetrating questions that catch his or her parents unaware, perhaps leaving them with feelings of rejection from the child.

The youngster, once viewed as "the chosen child" who gained a family, soon begins to realize that in the gaining there once had to be a "losing."

Communicating about adoption is not a one-time event. It is a process cultivated by the fulfillment of two requirements on the part of the parents. The first requirement is that parents have a clear perception of what adoption means to them. They must answer the question of the primary dilemma—"How do we see our family?" The second requirement is that parents comprehend how their child feels and thinks about being adopted by learning the developmental stages of understanding characteristic of an adopted child.

After these requirements are met, a family can dig into the nuts and bolts of communicating about adoption to their youngster, whether the adoption occurred in infancy or later on.

HOW DO WE SEE OUR FAMILY, AND WHAT DOES ADOPTION MEAN TO US?

REJECTION OF DIFFERENCES

It was not an unusual occurrence for ten-year-old Julie to play dress-up in the family attic on rainy days. However, on one particular day, Julie opened an unfamiliar trunk filled with all sorts of memorabilia. As Julie later related, what she found there turned her world upside down:

> Being naturally curious, I began looking through that trunk. I found a tiny little box filled with notecards. I opened it up and inside was a lamb-shaped card that said, "We have adopted a baby girl."
>
> I can remember standing there saying, *Dear Lord, let it be Susan, not me.* But it said, "We have adopted a brand-new baby girl, Julie Lynn."
>
> My world caved in. I couldn't believe it. I put it right back in the box.
>
> I was very teary for a number of days. Finally my

mother asked me what was the matter. I told her I found something in the attic. She asked me what I could have found in the attic that could make me so upset. I began to tell her what I discovered and she replied, "It's the truth. It *is* what we've done."

"Why didn't you tell me?" I pleaded.

Mother quietly replied, "I probably never would have told you." Later that afternoon, she told me more family secrets — my sister was adopted, one of my cousins was adopted. Everything changed for me that day.

Julie's parents faced a critical crossroads as they began their family. All adoptive families face that same crossroads. They must ask and answer pivotal questions. "As we raise this child, do we acknowledge the differences in our relationship created by adoption? Do we reject them and maintain the profile of a genetically related unit? Is there a balance between the two?"

According to adoption expert David Kirk, "some couples in reacting to their role handicap of adoptive parenthood (due to infertility), try to take the 'sting' out of adoption by simulating non-adoptive families as closely as possible."[1] In relating to their child, "they communicate the importance of forgetting about being adopted and all that goes with it — as they themselves try to do."[2] Kirk calls this style of managing adoption the rejection of differences.

Such a perspective works only for a time and meets the needs only of the adoptive parents. Kirk suggests that this rejection pattern potentially blocks "the development of an accepting and trusting family atmosphere — an atmosphere conducive to open, honest exploration of adoption-related issues."[3]

Candy, now an adult, recalls with anguish the lack of communication in her adoptive home about issues that were important to her. It left a deep void in her life:

My parents lost their only birth child to an unexplained illness when she was seven. Three years after her death, they adopted me. I was an infant. When I was six, my parents told me I was adopted. I still remember "the talk."

In later years if I asked my mother questions about adoption, she would get upset and say, "Don't worry about those things now. We don't talk about it. You are our little girl now."

Early in my teen years I knew that being adopted wasn't the "normal" thing. I convinced myself that since no one talked about it—or if they did it was in hushed tones—it must be a "bad thing." No one ever answered my questions. It was like the adoption never occurred.

Dr. Brodzinsky comments about the rejection or denial of differences coping style:

It is simply not dealing with the issues that the child deals with.

The child says, "I feel bad because my parents didn't want me."

The parents say, "Don't worry about that, honey, we love you."

. . . It is not so much a behavior, but a series of behaviors that create an atmosphere in which they are not fostering discussions about adoption. They ignore adoption-related issues. When there is an opportunity to talk about it, they choose not to. They sidestep the issues and discourage the child from talking about it.

I have had kids come to me directly and comment, "When I asked a question, Mom or Dad would say, that's not important now. You are with us." It's that kind of denial of differences we see. It gives the child the message that there is an act of betrayal on his part in talking about, wondering about, or being curious about being adopted.[4]

Motivation for adapting this particular approach, relates Brodzinsky, is threefold. First, it may be an attempt on the parents' part to minimize their sense of pain around loss. Second, they may also be hoping to protect the child from feeling that pain. Third, in some cases the parents are trying to protect themselves from potential loss—not the loss of the child, but the loss of the child's love and commitment to them.

ACKNOWLEDGMENT OF DIFFERENCES

A contrasting approach to rejecting differences is acknowledging them. Parents who choose this pattern remove the bondage of secrecy. They grant each family member the freedom to question and explore the range of issues and feelings that may surface throughout a lifetime.

Shelly recalled:

> One afternoon when I was about seven, my mother got my baby book down from the shelf. She called me over to sit down beside her. I knew that I was adopted; it seemed like I had always known. However, what she did that day opened doors for me in terms of finding out what I needed to know. As I grew older, I walked through those doors she opened that day—many, many times.
>
> While we skimmed the pictures, she pointed to the hospital where I was born. She told me more details of my birth and what it was like to come get me at seven days old and bring me home. She told me that they believed that God was a part of the whole process. Mom explained that my birth mother had made an adoption plan for me and that she picked their family for me. She ended our brief dis-cussion with words I later recalled when issues confronted me: "If you ever, ever have any questions or need to talk to us about any of this, we will always be there for you."
>
> My parents' willingness to talk openly about things that concerned my adoption provided a healthy, realistic, and honest foundation upon which to build my identity and self-worth.

Guatemalan-born Timothy joined the Myatt family when he was four months old. Tim and Traci never dreamed of having birth children. Yet just five months after Timothy arrived home, Traci discovered she was pregnant with their first birth child, Taylor. Eighteen months later, Tessa was born. Tim and Traci are just now experiencing the unique differences created by adoption. Timothy is asking questions.

A grocery store experience heightened their awareness of the differences. As Traci walked through the store with all three of her young children in the cart, a woman next to her admired the children. She then asked a question that imprinted itself on Timothy's young mind: "Where did you get him?" Traci didn't realize he had heard it until later.

That night as Tim was leaving little Timothy's bedroom after a time of story reading, Timothy blurted out, "Daddy, I don't know where I came from!"

"It just leveled me," Tim said. "I thought, *Oh no, it's starting already.* We had just been reading the story of Peter Pan, so I proceeded to tell him that he came from a place as beautiful as never-neverland — a place called Guatemala. He asked me where I came from; I told him Pennsylvania. He asked me where Mommy came from; I told him Kentucky. Those answers seemed to satisfy his three-year-old heart."

One struggle Tim foresees as a parent, in addition to dealing with the coping styles of rejecting versus acknowledging differences, is walking the fine line between convincing Timothy that he is special while not implying that he is privileged:

> It is a fine line, because I don't want to damage the relationship I have with Taylor and Tessa by giving special privileges to Timothy in an attempt to convince him he is special. Even now, I find myself evaluating what I do — I want to treat him as I would any birth child in things like discipline and responsibilities. At the same time, we want to give him the extra support that will help him get through the struggles of being adopted. Denying differences and acknowledging them is something like a juggling act.

There are many benefits in the style of acknowledging differences, assert professionals in the field. Both parents and professionals point out that this style is especially valuable in creating an environment of empathy and sensitivity in which feelings can be not only expressed but recognized as legitimate.

Five other advantages to this acknowledgment approach are noteworthy.[5] First, *it builds a trusting relationship between parent and child.* Lauren, now twenty-one, didn't learn she was adopted until her parents told her at age twelve: "I was traumatized by that disclosure — not so much for the adoption part, but that they had kept secrets from me. I have grown up wondering what else they haven't shared."

Second, this open style *integrates missing pieces from the child's past.* For many adopted children, lack of information creates a sense of a void in their life. Some say it's like trying to put a puzzle together, knowing you don't have all the pieces. Research has shown that children whose parents were open about adoption issues are generally more satisfied with the quality of family communication and relationships.

Third, *open disclosure corrects erroneous views of the past* as, fourth, *it helps the child sort out realities and fantasies.* "One of the greatest fantasies I maintained as a school-age child was that one day my now-rich birth parents would regret getting rid of me and come back for me," commented twenty-seven-year-old Diane. "I think I embellished that fantasy because I didn't have any clue of what was reality."

Fifth, this straightforward approach *helps form a foundation for identity formation.* A broader discussion of this critical adolescent need is addressed in chapter 10.

"Rejection of differences" and "acknowledgment of differences" represent two extremes. Is it possible to develop an approach somewhere in the middle? Dr. David Brodzinsky suggests how:

> Parents have to create a balance between talking about adoption and living life as a normal family. One way to do that is to ask oneself, "When was the last time we talked about it?" If a parent can't remember, there is probably a need to address it in some way.

Approaching it directly by telling a child to sit down and talk about adoption, cautions Brodzinsky, will probably be an unsuccessful effort. Finding less direct methods will meet with a more positive response.

Brodzinsky encourages parents to plant seeds. For example, a parent might open with the following:

> I was watching a TV show last night. It was interesting. It had a story about a birth mom who planned an adoption for her child. It reminded me a lot about your story. I've been thinking about it and wondering if you have had any thoughts or questions lately that we need to talk about.

This plants in the child's mind, *It's okay to talk about adoption in this home.*

A second suggestion (discussed more fully in the following chapter) is the use of books. A parent might say:

> I was at the bookstore the other day and there was a book about adoption. It is for kids your age. I bought it for you. Would you like to sit down with me and read it together or would you like to read it on your own?

In the early years of family life, when the primary job is to incorporate the child into the family and build connection and trust, a rejection of differences style may serve the family well, Brodzinsky says. Later on, as the young person matures and struggles to find meaning in being adopted and of relinquishment, an acknowledgment of differences pattern offers a clearer choice to ensure openness, honesty, and meeting needs.[6]

One final approach is found in some adoptive families. It differs from the first two in its consistently negative effects.

INSISTENCE UPON DIFFERENCES

"Carrie is an LD student because she is adopted."

"Joe was suspended a third time. I think the reason he's always in trouble is because he was adopted. He's a bad seed."

"If we had never adopted him, this family wouldn't be in such chaos. He came from such a terrible family."

All three of these statements reflect a third coping style, found in troubled adoptive families: "insistence upon differences." This management technique is found in families in crisis. Brodzinsky comments, "This pattern often leads family members to view adoption as the basis for family disharmony and disconnectedness."[7] It also relieves everyone—except the adopted child—of responsibility for any problem.

Of the three coping patterns potentially integrated into the family, this paradigm builds walls between parent and child and between adopted child and birth child. It reinforces to a struggling youngster that in this home he is expendable.

This view often leads families not into therapy, but into either an emotional disengagement or a courtroom to dissolve the adoptive relationship.

At age seven, Jesse is back in the foster care system. At age nine, Bonnie was returned to a foster home. At age seventeen, Todd walked out of his adoptive home. He will soon move into an independent living program and eventually move on into adulthood with very few stable family ties.

These three children were adopted at an early age. However, for a variety of reasons, their families were never able to incorporate and love them unconditionally. Symptoms of potential disruption occurred early, for with every problem or crisis the family would insist upon the differences.

In good times, Bonnie's parents introduced her as their daughter. In difficult times, an adjective was added—their "adopted" daughter. Their personal needs as parents and their inability or unwillingness to see the issues in the light of the whole family system brought heartache and disruption. Eventually, the walls that had been built over a period of time became insurmountable. No one had energy left to keep the relationships intact.

"We usually find very little of this insistence of differences until the kids begin to act out," says Brodzinsky:

> We find it mostly with families of teenagers who have a long history of parent-child conflicts, not necessarily around adoption issues, just a lot of acting out.
>
> When a family begins to look at all the problems in the family through the lens of adoption, that is when they get into this insistence of differences pattern. Adoption

then becomes the explanatory mechanism for explaining problems, and the only one. It then comes as no big surprise when an underlying message is given to the child, "you are adopted—of course you will have problems."[8]

Within this kind of family system, members internalize a belief system that takes on a life and energy of its own. That belief system is that adoption creates problems. Brodzinsky suggests, "insistence of differences is not what created the problem in the first place. But once the problems begin to emerge, the belief system begins to become a larger part of the parent and child relationship. This perception helps to maintain an atmosphere of non-acceptance, and therefore helps to maintain a level of on-going conflict."[9]

In most cases, this pattern does not lead to a formal dissolution of the relationship. More often, it leads to unrelenting conflict and a dissolution of any real sense of relationship and intimacy between the parents and child—unless professional help is sought.

Professional intervention in adoptive families in crisis is crucial. It helps the family to approach the problems as a unit and to separate those actions and behaviors that initiate conflict from the deeper belief system that maintains the struggle.

As parents fulfill the first requirement—evaluating how they see themselves as an adoptive family—they can prepare to complete the second requirement: to learn how their child feels and thinks about being adopted. They need to become acquainted with the developmental stages of understanding frequently observed in an adopted child.

HOW DOES THE CHILD PERCEIVE THE ADOPTION TIE?

As children mature, they grow in their understanding of what adoption means to them. Betsy Keefer and Judy Emig of the Parenthesis Post Adoption Project in Ohio have described this growing understanding in their study of developmental issues, which provides the basis for the following discussion.[10]

Each developmental stage ushers in a deeper perception of

the experience. Children ask more questions that invite parental sensitivity. Although these developmental stages are linked to chronological ages, every child is different. Some progress rapidly from one stage of understanding to another; others may remain at a particular stage much longer than expected. Still others may be significantly delayed, still demonstrating a lack of mature developmental understanding into their late teens or early twenties.

STAGE ONE—PRESCHOOL YEARS, AGES TWO TO FIVE
In this preliminary stage of an adopted child's life, she learns her "chosen baby story." Parents take great delight in telling the child of her "special" status. Young children sense in this loving, nurturing context the positive dimension of adoption.

Most parents enjoy hearing their youngster recite her adoption story. Although she usually can repeat it word for word, she has little understanding of its true meaning.

When five-year-old, Korean-born Whitney Casey answers the question "Where were you born?" she enthusiastically proclaims, "The Los Angeles Airport." Her parents have told her many times of the exciting day when she arrived from a land far away.

Lois Melina, adoptive parent and author, suggests three goals for parents in this stage. First, *acquaint the child with adoption terms rather than adoption concepts*. Second, *use the time to create a positive environment where adoption can be discussed*. Third, *become comfortable with talking about it*.[11]

STAGE TWO—EARLY ELEMENTARY YEARS, AGES FIVE TO EIGHT
As adopted children enter this period of their life, their understanding of adoption goes through significant change. Children at this age become more reflective, analytical, and logical in their thinking. "As a part of this growth in cognitive and social-cognitive reasoning," Brodzinsky explains, "children's knowledge of adoption also undergoes important changes."[12]

In the early elementary years, children begin to see a difference in how a child may enter his family: some enter by birth; others by adoption. They begin to understand "blood ties" or the lack of them. They begin to grasp that by gaining a family there had to be a losing. They initiate questions about the story. "This new knowledge may undermine a child's sense of security," Brodzinsky points out. "In the elementary years, children view adoption not only in terms of family building, but also in terms of family loss."[13]

This perception of relinquishment can be accompanied by many behavioral, emotional, and attitudinal changes. Research has shown that by the time adopted children reach the age of eight, many experience considerable ambivalence about being adopted.[14] Professionals working with children in this range describe some change in behavior related to the early feelings of insecurity and confusion.

STAGE THREE—LATE ELEMENTARY, AGES NINE TO TWELVE

When heading into the latency years, many adopted children seem to "go underground" about issues—they cease to ask questions and seem relatively unconcerned about the past.

Much may be happening inside, however. The youngster really begins to understand that his situation is different from his classmates. He begins to focus more on the thought that in order for the adoption to have happened, he had to have been given away.

Middle childhood is often characterized as a worry-free time with few responsibilities as youngsters focus on learning new skills, such as sports, or join exciting new activities, such as scouts or 4-H. However, there is a flip side to this carefree time:

> The more worrisome serious period is usually experienced in children's inner lives, as indicated by their dreams and fantasies. There their feelings are played out about themselves and their families. They wish to belong outside of this particular family circle. They desire to have attributes that make others admire them and seek them out. They develop fears that they are dumb, useless, mean and ugly.[15]

A child's self-image in this age bracket may be that he is "bad," "cheated," and a "throwaway."

Running through the hearts of adopted children is a sense

of what might have been regarding their birth family. This grief shows itself in different behaviors. Children who know that their birth parents made an adoption plan and who do not have a lot of meaningful information about their birth parents often struggle with low self-esteem and unworthiness. They feel devalued among their peers.

Lynn, a fifth grader, knew she was adopted. She never expressed much about her adoption. But new, troubling questions began to arise in her mind, and the insecurity manifested itself in her behavior.

Her adoptive mom, Carlotta, commented:

> We noticed that Lynn starting doing something that was noisome. She began to pull out her eyelashes, just out of nervousness. I quizzed her about what was going on. She always replied, "Nothing." So we just waited.
>
> One evening, long after she had gone to bed, Lynn tiptoed into the living room with tears streaming down her face.
>
> "Mommy, I want to ask you something," she told me, "but I don't want to make you mad. What does my birth mom look like? What did I do to make my birth mommy get rid of me? Can I see my real mommy?"
>
> I knew to expect these questions sooner or later. I encouraged Lynn by affirming that she was okay in asking those things of me. As a family, we sat down to watch a video we had placed aside of Lynn and Pat's birth family. She was able to see what her birth mother and grandparents looked like. It was an extremely positive experience for her. I also told her, "Some day, I will help you locate her. But for now we will just have to wait."

These late elementary years are apparently the time when many adopted children directly face the down side of adoption: the meaning of relinquishment. More and more agencies around the country are developing special groups just for children in this age range. The groups consist of other adopted children around their age and are often led by adolescents and adults who were adopted themselves. Talking to those leaders provides a positive glimpse into the future for these preteens.

STAGE FOUR — JUNIOR AND SENIOR HIGH SCHOOL

Every child entering this stage of development experiences many emotional, physical, and behavioral changes. When the struggle for adolescent independence runs headlong into parental control and structure, anger and frustration generally erupt.

Occasionally, adopted teens direct this anger at their parents, using "You're not my real mom" darts as a weapon against a vulnerable parent.

Adolescents are preoccupied at this age with two issues: "Who am I?" and "What will my future be?" For adopted teens, the questions are of greater intensity: "Who am I *really*? Can I have a future if I don't know my past?" They also add a third: "How did I really get separated from my family?"

As a result of the internal struggles, professionals and parents note behavioral changes that go beyond that of normal adolescent rebellion. They cite such things as anger and aggression, oppositional behavior, uncommunicativeness, self-image problems, substance abuse, truancy, school failure, temper outbursts (boys), depression (girls), and overreaction to rejection and loss from dating experiences. (Chapter 10 examines in great detail the adopted child in adolescence.)

STAGE FIVE — AGE SEVENTEEN THROUGH YOUNG ADULTHOOD

An adopted teenager in the latter years of this second decade of life comes down from a difficult period to enter a quieter stage. Anger has lessened, and the young adult refocuses on going on with life. He deals in greater urgency with the need to separate from his family, establish new peer relationships, and develop a vocational plan.

This is often the stage in which adopted kids decide to activate a search for their birth parents, seeking either information or a contact.

The young adult's greatest need in this developmental stage of growth is to fit in, to be like everyone else. Parents can support their child through this transition stage by continuing to work on resolving any tentative concerns left from an earlier period in his or her life (see chapter 10). The child will then experience a growing desire to put aside the sensitivities and vulnerabilities that were part of the adoption experience throughout childhood and live like others his age.[16]

Walking with a child through the developmental stages of adoption requires sensitivity to feelings and thoughts. For parents, it is helpful to know just how children really feel about being adopted. The following excerpts provide actual statements from adopted children.

HOW IT FEELS TO BE ADOPTED:
SPECIAL COMMENTS FROM SPECIAL CHILDREN

Valerie, age eleven (adopted at four weeks)
How do I feel about being adopted? Most of the time, I feel okay. My mom and dad and two sisters are my family. Every once in a while, I feel sad just for a little while. Just lately I have been thinking about being adopted. I sometimes wonder what my birth mom looks like. When I have questions, I want to go to my mom, but I don't want to hurt her feelings. I wonder, do I have other brothers and sisters somewhere? Maybe someday I will know.

**Nicki, age thirteen (adopted at nine, leaving behind
a long history of severe neglect)**
How does it feel to be adopted? I feel like I have always lived with my parents since I was born. A lot of people ask me how it feels to be adopted. It is a normal family. I know that I am safe and secure. My parents love me lots. I don't have to worry as much or be embarrassed as much. I didn't get to go to school before, but now I go all the time. That's how I feel. I never really think of my birth parents. The only time is when someone asks me.

Soo-Mee, age eight (adopted at three from Korea)
We have some pictures of the day I arrived in New York from Korea. I came with five other children, and a nun and two priests took care of us on the plane. I have a photograph of my mom at the airport hugging me and looking very happy. I was three

years old. . . . I wish I could remember my real-real-real parents and know what they look like, but the Mommy I have is terrific and I love her a lot.[17]

Lisa, age eleven (entered adoptive home at seven from a neglectful, abusive birth family)
I love being adopted. I feel safe and comfortable living here and I know I will never be taken away. I will always have this loving family.

At first I felt scared. After four years of staying with them I know this is the family I am supposed to be in. I really never think about my birth parents very much or how it was back then. I have fun here. I don't have as many problems as I used to have. I know I have a mom and a dad by my side all the time.

Alex, age seven (entered adoptive home at three)
I love my family.

SUMMARY

When preparing to communicate with children about their adoption, it is important that parents fulfill two requirements:

1. Honestly evaluate what adoption means to them as parents and how they see their family. Do they deny the differences, acknowledge the differences, or find a balance between the two? Do they insist on the differences when confronting problems within the relationship?

2. Comprehend how their child feels and thinks about being adopted, and learn the developmental stages of understanding frequently observed in an adopted child. Parents must also be sensitive to the feelings accompanying each stage in their children's lives.

QUESTIONS FOR SMALL GROUPS

1. What are your needs in this adoption experience? Will you deny the differences adoption creates in order to meet those needs?

2. What else can you do to balance the two approaches of denying and accepting the differences?

3. What have you observed in adoptive families who insist on the differences?

4. Have you observed your child experiencing any of the developmental stages listed in this chapter? Have you had any particular problems with these developmental issues?

CHAPTER EIGHT

Talking to Children About Adoption:

When and How

What is the best place to start when talking to a child about his life
and about adoption? The best place is the beginning.
A child's life did not begin at the time of adoption.
The youngster has a unique history all his own that he is entitled to know.
Family Ties

B eth is now twenty-one years old and she is still angry. Her parents died in an automobile accident when she was twelve. After their death, she was told by her grandmother that she was adopted. At her most fragile developmental stage, this preteen suffered the most incredible losses a young person could experience. She lost both of her parents. She also lost all concept of who she was and where she came from.

Perhaps the most delicate dilemma of the adoptive parent-child relationship is the need to communicate to children about their past. If a child enters the family as an infant, creating an environment of openness to share this vital information is the primary task. If a child is older at the time of adoption, parents must help inform the child about the facts in his or her past and also aid in the healing of memories.

When should parents tell children they were adopted? How much should they tell them? How do parents deal with a child's past? How can parents help heal any unpleasant memories the child may have brought with him?

These questions present parents with a potentially stressful assignment. However, if parents understand the reasons behind what they must do and have the tools to accomplish the task, it can be a process that binds the relationship of promise more tightly together.

WHEN TO TELL CHILDREN THEY WERE ADOPTED: TWO PERSPECTIVES

"WAIT UNTIL LATER"

In recent years, there has been a limited controversy over the pros and cons of early communication with a child about adoption.

Dennis Donovan, M.D., and psychologist Deborah McIntyre, coauthors of *Healing the Hurt Child*, believe that early disclosure cripples a child's ability to form close relationships. "Studies have shown that adopted children are more than twice as likely as the rest of the population to be in therapy."[1] They also noted that these adopted children mirrored similar emotional difficulties, such as hoarding food or nursing wounds of a negative self-image. From these observations, the duo conclude, "there has to be something inherent in the adoptive situation that causes the same problems over and over."[2]

Donovan places the blame squarely on the problem of telling children about adoption too early in their lives. Preschool children, he feels, do not have the proper development of cognitive skills or ability to understand the information they are given about adoption.

These professionals argue against early disclosure for several reasons: First, parents should concentrate on forming loving, trusting relationships within the family unit. If adoption is a topic, it could potentially negate that security. Second, children often blame themselves for the adoption. They develop the belief that their sickness or behavior caused their parents to give them away, and they lack the cognitive skills to filter out such faulty logic. Third, young children are "unable to balance in their minds the double meaning of adoption—being unwanted by birth parents and wanted by adoptive parents."[3]

Because of these convictions, Donovan and McIntyre recommend that the adoption should not be mentioned unless the child asks questions. Then they support disclosure of honest, accurate information. McIntyre says, "We simply believe that the information should not come when the parents want to tell, but when the child wants to know."

"TELL THEM EARLY"

A large majority of adoptive parents and professionals strongly disagree with the "wait until later" approach. They have found no validation of McIntyre's claims that it creates tremendous insecurity and self-blame at that early age because children do not have cognitive understanding of it.

Most adoption experts encourage parents to tell them early. A variety of reasons guide their perspective.

Tom and Gail Burton, adoptive parents of two children (Erin, seven, and Brooke, four), had decided to wait to tell them about their adoption until they were in junior high school. Everyone from great-grandmother to aunts and uncles promised to carry the "secret"; however, someone forgot to clue in the cousins.

During a family reunion, Erin and a cousin got into a squabble over which youngster could stay with grandmother first.

"I know that Grandmother wants me first," Judi shouted. "You're not one of us; my mom said you're adopted!"

In choosing to postpone talking to Erin and Brooke, these parents relinquished control of the "secret." They abdicated their responsibility to mere risk, leaving Erin and Brooke vulnerable to the winds of circumstances.

Regrettably, some factions of society today continue to devalue adoption by viewing it as second best. When parents gamble with the disclosure of adoption they leave it potentially in the hands of thoughtless acquaintances or insensitive family members. The information may then be given in a cruel, tactless manner.

"When it comes from the outside, it is often an attack," says Paul Brinick, Ph.D., associate professor of psychology at the University of North Carolina.[4] Children often carry the scars from such a traumatic revelation well into adulthood.

Parents who choose to disclose adoption early, during the toddler and preschool years, set the tone for the lifelong journey on a firm footing. This attitude promotes a healthy parent-child relationship in three ways.

First, the parents are the first ones to create awareness of adoption within the context of their love and commitment. They know that although a toddler may not understand the words, the spirit in which they are said is crucial.

Second, they will offer honest, accurate information, thus avoiding the necessity of attempting to "undo" someone's mismanagement of the facts.

Third, these parents will not have to live under the shadow of secrecy and the fear of accidental revelation.

CREATING AN ENVIRONMENT
WHERE QUESTIONS CAN BE ASKED AND ANSWERED

Whether children are adopted as infants or as older youngsters, there will be multiple periods in their life when they will deal with separating from their first family.

For an older child who has memories of that family, a keener awareness of that loss is apparent and is occasionally recalled. A supportive approach in walking the child through those periods of questions and confusion can be found in the use of two vital communication tools — bibliotherapy and the life book.

USING LITERATURE TO EXPLAIN ADOPTION
Bibliotherapy simply means "helping with books." It refers to the use of selected literature to help children broaden their total development.[5] Through the employment of literature relevant to adoption issues, children can see how other youngsters in similar circumstances confronted difficulties and overcame them. They can also see how children just like them faced disappointments, fears, failures, and successes. They can apply what they learn to their own situations.

Adoptive parents are the ideal candidates for using literature in the warmth of the home to lead a child through a particularly difficult stage. In preparing to do this, parents should be aware of three criteria when choosing reading materials for their children: age, reading level, and special needs of the child.[6]

When selecting books, chronological age and reading level are obvious considerations. Children relate well when reading or hearing stories of others their age. Reading interests of preschoolers are kindled by stories with colorful pictures and simple dialogue. Older elementary children enjoy stories that develop character and plot. The adolescent can be helped with books that cover concerns relevant to adopted teens such as parent-teen struggles, identity crises, or decisions about moral values or career choices.

Choosing reading material for a child with special needs could revolve around such apprehensions as leaving a foster family, loss of siblings, living in a transcultural family, or birth order realignment.

Books can provide an emotional release for children who are wrestling with personal issues. To maximize the productivity of the reading, parents must learn how to explore feelings and attitudes by asking appropriate and timely questions. (At the end of this chapter is a suggested reading list of books that can be helpful in this effort.)

THE LIFE BOOK — THE BRIDGE FROM AN UNKNOWN PAST TO A PROMISING FUTURE

"I don't have any memories of the important people in my past. I wonder if the important people in my past have any memories of me."[7]

Each child's reaction to the separation from his family of origin presents its own set of unique, individual responses. But these painful feelings weave a common thread throughout the lives of older adopted children. For children whose memories of former relationships smolder vaguely in their minds, frequent themes revisit during the healing process:[8]

- Feelings of abandonment accompanied by feelings of humiliation and worthlessness
- Anger at the person who deserted them either by surrender, death, or divorce

- Feelings of being responsible for the desertion, in total disregard of reality
- Shame or guilt about the terrible "deed" they believe caused the separation
- A need to punish oneself for such a deed

For children to move from a painful past to a promising future, they must have an understanding of past and present events and why things happened as they did. According to Marian Parker, a ten-year veteran in adoption services with the Hamilton County (Ohio) Department of Human Services, "this understanding is vital for [the child's] sense of identity, his sense of continuity, and most all, his sense of worth." The most effective tool for helping children to integrate their past into their present is a retrospective of their life in words and pictures.

The Purpose for the Life Book
The basic purpose for the life book is to provide answers to questions that are as yet unasked. Therefore its content must contain clear, accurate information. Marian Parker makes the following recommendations:

> It is essential that we tell the child the truth — at least, as much of the truth as he is able to understand at his level of development. It is crucial that the truth be told with compassion for all those involved. In describing the negative aspects of a child's life, words must be chosen with great care and sensitivity. Sensationalism must be avoided at all times. The child may well wish to share his life book with people important to him . . . and we must make every effort to ensure that he is able to do so with reasonable comfort and minimal embarrassment.
>
> This is not to say that the realities of his life should be sugarcoated . . . but rather that our manner of narrating these realities should show compassion for the human limitations that caused him to be neglected, abused, abandoned, or whatever. We need to convey to the child

that the bad things that have happened to him are not a reflection of his worth, and most important, that they were not his fault. Above all, we need to convey to him our hope that better things are coming.[9]

What Goes into the Life Book?
The exact content of a child's life book should reflect his unique life story. Most public agencies now provide adoptive parents with a child study inventory that includes a non-identifying social and medical history of the parents. Adoptive parents should ask for such information if it is not made available. In foster care adoptions, foster parents are often acquainted with the birth family and have access to more extensive information. In private adoptions, comprehensive details rarely are gathered.

Whatever portion of it can be obtained, the following information will become an invaluable treasure for the adopted child at some point in the future:

1. Child's birth information: date, time, location (city, state, hospital), weight, and height.
2. Child's family tree: genogram. (A genogram resembles a family tree. It is a more detailed description of family members over an extended period of time. It can be helpful in preserving information such as births, deaths, separations, ethnic backgrounds, and medical history.) The genogram should include date of parents' birth, physical description of parents, education and employment of parents, known health problems of parents, grandparents, and siblings.[10]
3. Foster homes or relatives' homes where the child has lived.
4. School-related information: list of schools attended, dates, teachers' names, report cards, comments from teachers, and sample work.
5. Medical information on the child.
6. Letters and mementos from parents, relatives, or significant others.
7. Anecdotes about the child: developmental milestones;

favorite activities, hobbies, or sports; favorite friends; cute, "naughty" behaviors; special trips or outings with the foster family; religious experiences.

Who Contributes to the Life Book?

The contents of the child's life book can come from several sources, according to Marian Parker.

Primary contributors to the life book in its initial stages are foster parents. They play a significant role in compiling, collecting, and preserving pictures and other documentation. They are usually the ones who carry the ongoing development of the book.

A second participant is the social worker. This person serves as a facilitator to the entire process and generally has access to the needed information.

The child, if age appropriate, should also be an active participant in what he or she wants in the book. Comments and drawings included in the book will have meaning later in the child's life.

Finally, other participants can be the birth parents and other relatives. The social worker is often able to gather content for the book from relatives of the child. Frequently, a birth parent writes a letter to the child that shares the hows and whys of difficulties that arose or decisions that necessitated the transfer of parental rights.

HOW TO ADDRESS SENSITIVE ISSUES

Lisa, Robin, and Terri joined other adoptive mothers at the life book workshop. Their assignment that day, with the help of agency staff, was to update their child's life book. For Lisa and Robin, the job was simple. Both of their children came into their families as infants, straight from the hospital. For Terri, the task was fragile, and it concerned her. Dale, their bright, happy two-year-old, came into their family as a result of a harsh reality. His mother was dead. His father had killed her. How does one write that in a child's life book?

Adoptive parents are genuinely concerned about dealing with sensitive issues regarding their child's past. So much of a child's sense of worth can still be tied to his family of origin. How a child perceives that family can shape his opinion of himself.

When wrestling with the fear of stirring things up, parents should be aware that it's not what is shared openly and honestly that agitates problems — it's the hidden secrets that leave a child unsettled and insecure.

The following suggestions may prove helpful when constructing a child's life story amidst negative circumstances. In each situation, adoptive parents must emphasize and reemphasize that *the child is not at fault regarding his circumstances,* that he did not create his birth parents' problems nor is he in any way responsible for them. They can also lead the child into an attitude of forgiveness. Parents should not condone or sugarcoat the behavior of the birth parents. However, in an effort to avoid bitterness taking hold within the child, they can encourage the child as he matures to "hate the sin, but forgive the sinner."

Realities are sometimes hard to face. Following are some of the difficult realities that many adopted children must confront, with sample ways to explain them to children.

EXPLAINING MENTAL ILLNESS

Your father was upset in his feelings and behavior. This often left him very confused. Because he couldn't handle the problems of his own life very well, it was impossible for him to provide you with a happy and safe home.

EXPLAINING ALCOHOLISM OR SUBSTANCE ABUSE

Your parents had many sad feelings that made life difficult for them. Because of those unhappy feelings, they would drink too much alcohol (or use drugs) to help them forget their problems.

They did not have control over their drinking (or drug use) and would often leave you in a dangerous situation. Because of their drinking habit, they could not guarantee a safe family home.

EXPLAINING LAWBREAKING

Sometimes, adults make bad decisions about how they will behave. There were times when your first mother chose to break the law. She thought that (name the crime) would help her to solve some of her problems. It did not.

Because of her bad choices, she had to spend time in jail. The judge decided that it was best for your mother to spend time in prison so that she could learn to make better decisions. Another judge also decided that the jail term would be too long a time for you to wait to be with a family so he asked a children's services agency (or whoever was responsible) to make an adoption plan for you.

EXPLAINING MENTAL RETARDATION
Some people are born with a thinking handicap that prevents them from learning as well or as quickly as other adults. Your mother had this problem. It was difficult for her to learn things like cooking, cleaning, and taking care of her personal needs. Many adults had to help her care for herself. It was too difficult for your birth mother to take care of herself and to learn how to care for you. She was unable to do both. Because of her inability to learn new things, she could not provide a safe home environment for you.

EXPLAINING ABANDONMENT
Your parents were very confused when you were born about how to care for you. They were frightened at the task of raising a baby, because they were still very young themselves (or they didn't have any money). They decided that it was best to leave you in the hospital (or whatever they did) when you were born, so that other, more responsible adults could make good decisions about your life. They knew that these people would do a good job of caring for you and that they would find a loving home.

EXPLAINING CHILD ABUSE
Your first parents often became frustrated, impatient, and angry over things. Instead of learning how to deal with what was bothering them, they took it out on you and hurt you. It is possible that their parents did the same things to them as they were growing up.

Because of the times they hurt you, the court officials decided that they were unable to be good parents and asked a children's service agency (or whoever was responsible) to make an adoption plan for you so that you could grow up happy and safe.

Explaining Sexual Abuse

Your father touched you in ways that were not right. He knew that what he was doing was not right for children. He and other adults may have told you to keep it a secret or that you were just imagining things. You were in no way responsible for his behavior. It was a good thing that you shared this secret with people who could help you get away from it.

HOW ONE ADOPTIVE FAMILY HANDLED
A DIFFICULT REALITY

Following the workshop, Terri felt more confident in writing about her son's history before he joined their family. This is what she wrote about the circumstances of his mother's death:

> Your father and mother had a great deal of trouble getting along with each other. They would often argue so loudly that neighbors worried about you.
>
> Eventually, your father moved out of the house that you lived in. He had problems dealing with his anger. He needed help from a counselor, but he didn't get it.
>
> One night, very late, he came over to your house. Your father became very angry with your mother. He began hurting her so badly that she died. Because of what he did, he will be in prison for a very long time. Maybe he can get the help he needs while he is there.

Terri and her husband also kept newspaper clippings of the tragic affair. When Dale is older and if he wishes more information about the whole matter, they will share it with him. They plan to do so for two reasons: it was a highly publicized event in a small community, and so, many residents know Dale's story.

Whatever circumstances created a difficult past for their

child, it is crucial for parents to deal with those realities. Facts create an environment of healing. Secrets block it. As children face the facts of their past, they will occasionally need to deal with the memories from those events. Those memories may spark mood changes and alter behavior.

HELPING THE MEMORIES HEAL:
RECOGNIZING ANNIVERSARY REACTIONS

Jackie came in from school one November afternoon and went straight to her room. She had been doing this all week. Her parents had become increasingly concerned, because normally she was a perky, happy-go-lucky junior-high student.

Jackie had joined their family four years earlier, when she was eight. Periodically, she had gone through these same withdrawal behaviors. It was time to find out what was happening inside her. They contacted her counselor the following morning.

What Daryl and Ruth found out resulted in real understanding not only on their part but also on Jackie's part. Jackie was experiencing an "anniversary reaction." She had been part of the foster care system since the age of three, when she had been removed from her birth family on a cold, dreary November day. She went to a foster home where she lived about a year.

On a snowy day just after Thanksgiving, Jackie's social worker came to the home and moved her to another foster family. From that point, Jackie was put through three additional moves, and all but one occurred in late fall.

Because Jackie and her parents had no knowledge of the dates of the moves, they never recognized the corresponding reaction. Now they knew that Jackie was emotionally responding to the anniversary of major separations in her life. When the weather turned cold, Jackie identified it with a move from one home to another and the onslaught of more grief and confusion.

Jackie's story is not unusual, according to Cincinnati psychotherapist Deborah Joy:

> Children often create distance in their close relationships in an unconscious attempt to avoid further loss. This

frequently occurs at anniversary times of separation or trauma in their lives. Some children feel anxious and begin to act out their feelings. Others become tearful and depressed.

Healthy adults who experience a major trauma, death, or separation often revisit grief in the years to come on the anniversary of when the crisis occurred. Imagine how these youngsters, who have not been responded to early in their times of deep suffering, deal with it.[11]

Joy says that these reactions are not limited to dates. Feelings and behavior can be triggered by such things as a person, an object, or an action. For example, the sight of a firefighter or police officer might remind a child of the person who removed her from her birth home. A particular type of discipline used in the adoptive home may send a child into an unexpected response.

When eighteen-month-old Lindsay came from her emergency foster home into her adoptive family, a critical piece of information was not given to her parents. Up to the time she entered foster care, Lindsay spent seven to ten daylight hours stuck in her crib. When her adoptive parents used the crib as a disciplinary measure during the daylight hours, Lindsay reacted hysterically. Had the parents known what the crib signified to Lindsay, they would never have used it.

In handling anniversary reactions, and eventually helping the child's memories to heal, Joy suggests the following:

- Obtain as much specific information about the daily life of the child as possible. Find out what time of year major events such as moves and separations occurred.
- Remember that negative behavior may signal emotional distress. Parents who understand what problems the behavior might be signaling will respond more appropriately.
- Work with a therapist who understands adoption issues. A third party is often very helpful for a family

who may lose objectivity in the middle of a crisis.
- Use the life book. It is one of the most helpful tools in bringing memories to the surface so that they can be dealt with and their negative power defused.

Confronting issues of a child's past through the life book and through therapy takes a great deal of sensitivity and work. One might ask, does all the work make a difference? Ask an adopted teenager.

IS THE LIFE BOOK WORTH THE EFFORT?

Myndi Breakfield was adopted in 1978 at age five. At that time, life books were not routinely suggested. Her adoptive parents saw the need and constructed Myndi's story for her as she entered adolescence. The following is her perspective, in the form of a letter written to her birth parents:

Dear Mom and Dad,
Do you remember me? You held me many times before you gave me up for adoption.
I do not remember you at all. I was only a year old when I knew you. I only know what my life book says about me, about you, and about my past.
You see, my parents adopted me when I was five. They also adopted two of my brothers. They were really patient in trying to help us accept them—they had as many fears as we had questions.
When my older brother turned sixteen, my parents prepared a life book for us. At that stage in life, we were all teens and our insecurities had set in. We wondered why we were adopted and who you were. We wondered if we had any siblings, what our pre-adoptive life was like. We even wondered what kind of medical problems were in our birth family.
My adoptive mother felt that the life book was so important to us that I remember she stayed up all night and had to call off work the next day in order to finish it.

She was scared that the truth would turn us away from her. She now knows how wrong she was.

The life book answered so many of my questions about you and even sparked interest in things that I had not known about myself. Within the pages of this book, I was able to discover and accept a secret part of my past that otherwise might have kept me troubled and confused for life.

Reality crept in as I was able to put an end to the fairy-tale dreams that many adopted girls have of being a long-lost heiress or princess. I finally came to terms with who you were. I found that I had an older brother and sister also, and the book informed me some about them.

My life book also told me of my medical past, with copies of doctor visits while in foster care and some of the medical past of my birth family.

The book explained reasons why we were removed from your home. That answer was so important to me. I no longer wonder why we were adopted. Before the life book, I would cry, wondering if I was just given up, unwanted, or abandoned. That book put an end to my tears.

I'm very glad my parents took the time to make the book for me so that I could know about you and my past. I am now able to accept who I am and seek out a better future because I know my past.

Love,
Your daughter,
Myndi

SUMMARY

One of the most important tasks undertaken by adoptive parents is communicating about their child's past. They must make a decision whether to postpone the telling or initiate it early in the child's life.

There are two specific tools that parents can develop for the task—bibliotherapy and the life book.

In addition to talking to their children about the facts of their past, parents should also help their children in the process of healing any hurts that resulted from it.

QUESTIONS FOR SMALL GROUPS
1. When do you think children should be told that they are adopted? Why?
2. What do you think are the strongest reasons supporting the "tell them early" approach?
3. What other kinds of comments or explanations are helpful for assisting children to understand the realities of their past?
4. What other materials can be added to a child's life book?

SUGGESTED READING MATERIAL FOR CHILDREN AND TEENS
These materials can be ordered through bookstores or borrowed from local libraries.

Angel, Ann. *Real for Sure Sister.* A newly adopted baby joins the household, and Amanda struggles to understand her own adoption experience. Ages five to ten.

Brodzinsky, Ann. *The Mulberry Bird.* Helps children understand why their birth mothers planned adoption for them. By using birds instead of children and their parents, the subject is presented from a gentle perspective.

Bunin, Sherry and Catherine. *Is That Your Sister?* A picture book about interracial adoption.

Joy, Deborah. *Benjamin Bear.* This story will relate to children whose life experiences of abuse or neglect preceded their adoption. Children play an active role with the one who is reading to them.

Livingston, Carole. *Why Was I Adopted?* A humorous book that addresses adoptive families with a great deal of love. It uses informal language and encourages a child to ask questions. Ages two to eight.

Okimoto, Jean. *Molly By Another Name*. Tackles critical questions for teenagers, such as questions surrounding a birth search and the effect that Molly's curiosity may have on her adoptive parents.

Rosenburg, Maxine. *Growing Up Adopted*. Adults and children alike share their personal stories about their adoption experiences, feelings, and opinions.

Schnitter, Jane. *William Is My Brother*. This is a story of blending birth children and adopted children. It explores differences, similarities, and feelings in a sensitive manner.

PART FOUR

Growing Up Adopted

CHAPTER NINE

Creating a Nurturing Family:
Giving Our Children What They Need

---

*Adoptive families differ from other families because of the circumstances
that brought them together. This unique family union generates
its own set of special concerns and its own special privileges.
Adoptive families should celebrate the value of their differentness.*
Family Ties

B ruce and Annie Schaffer beamed with pride as their daughter Alissa walked to the platform to receive her high school diploma. Alissa had come to them at just three weeks old. The years had flown by for this loving family. As they reflected over the many, many joys of raising Alissa and their other two adopted children, they were thankful for the direction life had taken them.

Home life at the Schaffers had not been without its challenges. At moments of crisis, just like every parent will do, Bruce and Annie questioned their parenting skill. Yet at heart, the Schaffers knew that they had, to the best of their ability, created a positive, nurturing environment where each child could grow and change to fulfill their inborn potential.

From the beginning of their relationship with these beautiful daughters and because of the special circumstances of their lives, the Schaffers had asked themselves a simple but significant question: "What do these children need?" From that initial consideration came a worthwhile parenting philosophy that continues to guide them as parents today.

WHAT DO THESE CHILDREN NEED?

TO BELONG

Stepping out of the car, Alissa turned to her parents. "My graduation day has been so special to me," she said. "You both have done so very much for me. Just recently I have had some real questions about what I was going to do with my life, and where am I really going from here. One thing I know — whatever I do, wherever I go, I do know to whom I truly belong."

In *The Gift of Honor*, psychologist Dr. John Trent describes the sense of belonging as the "need each person has to feel a special, needed and important part of the family . . . children who grow up with a strong sense of belonging gain ground on those who don't. Seeds of acceptance sown in children give them the ability to give and receive love and acceptance later on in life."[1]

Children removed from their families of origin are already a step or more behind in that needed emotional foundation. The task for adoptive parents is to create a family environment where their children gain the sense of belonging, of being wanted and loved. There are numerous ways this can be accomplished.

Building Blocks of Belonging

Block 1. Names are significant in developing a sense of belonging to a child. For an infant, the family has the privilege of giving the child his or her chosen name. For an older child whose identity is already attached to his or her name, adding a middle name of family significance promotes belonging.

Block 2. Belonging comes through being the recipient of legitimate praise and affirmation. This affirmation comes in all sizes and shapes:

- Warm hugs and physical closeness
- Time spent with a child reading the same book for the fifth time

- Verbal affirmation of a job well done
- Small gestures, such as a note in a lunch box or the preparation of a special dinner or dessert

Block 3. Belonging comes through active listening. This statement may seem obvious, but it is more often neglected than realized. Dr. Trent points out that "the healthiest families are those who score high in the area of listening. Most of us are better lecturers than we are listeners. Even when we listen, it often is just a pause between bursts of what's really important—what we have to say."[2]

Block 4. We build a sense of belonging into the hearts of our children through a well-defined purpose for the family. So often families live, eat, and sleep under the same roof yet enjoy very little depth in their relationships.

A well-defined purpose for the family can include working toward goals together. Goals cement relationships. Activities might include planning special holiday celebrations, learning a new skill or hobby together, visiting a nursing home together, or getting involved in a community project that requires giving of oneself.

Just like adults, children need to be needed. A family that is dedicated to a common purpose can satisfy that desire.

Block 5. Children learn that they belong to a family when they feel free to express their feelings appropriately. Insecure adopted children often mask their true feelings in order to ensure acceptance. Parents who encourage children to share their feelings and learn to draw those feelings forth deepen their sense of belonging.

The consequences of growing up without this sense of belonging can be severe. Dr. Trent cites such problems as the inability to give and receive love, procrastination in responsibility, inability to handle relational conflicts, and stress of any magnitude—to name just a few.

Children growing up in adoptive families not only need the sense of belonging instilled deep within them, but they need to be shown that they have permission to be an individual in their own right.

TO BE AUTHENTIC

Rachel sat in her high school counselor's office as they discussed her plans for college.

"I really would like to go into teaching," Rachel said, "but both Dad and Mom have their hearts set on nursing for me. All the women in our family are nurses. I've told them I don't want to do that, but they just don't seem to listen."

Rachel is the daughter of Frank and Millie Fields. She was adopted into their family as an infant. After they lost two babies through miscarriage, Rachel's presence was sheer joy to them.

The Fields' plans for Rachel were full of high expectations. They counted on her achieving in school and eventually following her mother's footsteps into a nursing program. The problem was that they never truly considered what Rachel wanted. Even more important, they never considered her innate capacities and preferences. They had molded her into what they wanted and she had complied.

"Loss of authenticity," states David Damico, "occurs when we are shaped and molded by the expectations of others who are trying to make us into someone they want us to be rather than allowing us to become who we really are."[3] Rachel felt that in order to maintain peace in the family, she was forced to play a role that would fit the dream of the children her parents had lost. More than anything, Rachel needed permission from her parents to grow into the person she was created to be—not into a fantasy child designed to be a parental replica.

The need to belong and the need to be authentic are two important factors in a healthy family environment. A third need of adopted children is to be given a sense of dignity.

TO HAVE A SENSE OF DIGNITY

Liz, Mick, and their two beautiful children from Korea sat in a restaurant waiting on their food order. Patrick (seven) and Megan (five) joined their families as infants and were the absolute delight of their lives. They usually attracted attention wherever they went.

That particular evening, a woman came over to the table and began to ask questions. "How old are your children? How long have they been with you?" Then the bomb dropped. "Why didn't their mother want them?" Both children stopped their chattering and looked at their mother. Liz simply said, "We have discussed that with the children." She felt no obligation to answer the woman's intrusive questions.

Many adopted children live under a looming shadow cast by rejection. There is no greater threat to a sense of dignity than to be rejected by birth parents. Uncaring, insensitive adults or childhood peers can continue to gnaw away at a child's sense of dignity by unkind remarks. What things can adoptive parents do to maintain a sense of dignity for their child?

1. *Start with building a strong moral, ethical, and spiritual environment.* A child will stand straighter and taller and face her world with stronger confidence when her family gives her a solid sense of right and wrong, sets loving boundaries, teaches her basic respect for herself and family members, and instructs her in the value of life.

2. *Learn to honor the child's heritage.* If the child is from a foreign country, celebrate the differences on occasions such as holidays or birthdays. Include neighborhood playmates and school friends in those celebrations.

3. *Avoid comparisons with other family members.* Comments such as "Why can't you be more like your brother?" tear down a child's sense of dignity.

4. *Support the child's efforts to achieve.* Don't humiliate a failure, as this father did. Joshua stayed after school each night for two weeks, telling his dad that he was getting help with math. Actually, he was trying out for the basketball team. Being shorter than his competitors, Joshua didn't make it. Eventually, his dad found out. The only comment he had was "What made you think you could make the team, anyway?" Joshua still carries the painful memory of his father's words.

To belong, to be authentic, to be given a sense of dignity—these elements are crucial in a positive, nurturing environment. There are two more.

TO BE VALUED

One critical block to a child receiving what he needs from a nurturing family, according to Dr. Trent, is the developmental freeze point at which many children are adopted. As a result of a series of abusive or neglectful life events, these children freeze in their ability to attach. They are emotionally blocked in their capacity to give or receive love because they lack any sense of personal value.

Dr. Trent commented from his experience in working with adoptive families:

> In those families where the parents became experts at extending "the family blessing" even through the roughest of waters, each individual in the home tended to do better and grow in attachment to one another. Struggles still came, but were handled in the environment of family security.[4]

As Dr. Trent defines it, the "family blessing" is the universally longed-for sense of unconditional affirmation. In the deepest part of our being, it is the sense that we are loved, respected, and valued as a person for who we are. It is not based on what we accomplish. It is, says Trent, a gift to us from our parents.

The elements of the blessing begin with *meaningful touch*. Families that do a great deal of hugging, touching, and playful wrestling are healthier families. Adoptive families may find that this step must be taken gradually for some children. For others, a lot of hugging begins the day together and ends it as well.

The components of the blessing continue with *spoken words that attach high value* to a person. The Bible says that "life and death are in the power of the tongue." Words have great power in themselves to encourage or destroy self-esteem.

Jessica, now an adult, was adopted as an infant into Carl and Rhonda's loving family. Handicapped with a disabling limp, Jessica did not play outside much but would spend hours "playing at" the piano. Her parents soon discovered her incredible talent. They encouraged her with words of enthusiasm and reminded her frequently of the wonderful gift of music she'd been given.

Jessica has rich memories of her parents' affirmations. "It is almost like they forgot my handicap. It was never an issue, merely a fact of life. What they saw was the potential they believed God had given me to play musical instruments."

The blessing is extended as parents or loved ones *picture a special future* for a child. This involves vocalizing the belief that each child is capable of success in some area of life.

The blessing is best fulfilled in an environment of active commitment in which parents become students of their children and work to see that a child is supported in reaching his or her potential.[5]

As parents provide the elements of the family blessing, adopted children can have the security and self-confidence to face their particular issues in a healthier way. They are not dependent on their birth parents' approval to mold the foundation of their lives.

In addition to the needs for belonging, authenticity, dignity, and a sense of value, there is a fifth important element of the family.

To Be Loved Unconditionally

Unconditional love is a concept taught in support groups, church workshops, and parenting classes. This key concept is necessary to provide children and teens with needed security. However, there is often a catch: The concept is taught, but the components of how to live it are not.

Components of Unconditional Love[6]

1. *Unconditional love risks rejection.* Parents who involve themselves in the life of the child they adopted must understand that their best intentions may be met head-on with rejection. Children who experience the loss of their birth parents or separation from significant foster parents do not rush headlong into other close relationships. These children arrive with a great deal of catching up to do.

Unconditional love wades into relationships with these children knowing that potential rejection is part of the process of learning to attach to a new family.

2. *Unconditional love permits negative feelings.* Parents of difficult teenagers often struggle with anger, frustration, disappoint-

ment, and numerous other difficult emotions. But these feelings are rarely communicated to the offender or to the other spouse in a healthy way. If they are not repressed, they are expressed in a manner that is later regretted.

Unconditional love allows those feelings to exist openly and encourages them to be expressed in a manner that will allow resolution.

3. *Unconditional love deals with reality.* Hoping to help a child avoid the pain of facing a struggling situation, parents sometimes cloud the truth with fantasy. They equate this with love.

If a child encounters problems at school, instead of admitting the child has a deficit and needs help, a parent may simply say the teacher can't teach. Thinking that it is easier for them as a parent to avoid issues from the child's past, parents run around questions, refusing to address them directly.

Unconditional love thrives in an environment where each family member honestly faces the problems of life with a determination to overcome obstacles.

4. *Unconditional love isn't manipulative and pushy.* Desiring to shape an adopted child to fit the portrait of that "dream child" leads parents into pushing a child into activities that are of no interest to him. They manipulate circumstances that benefit only "the dream."

This message comes through loud and clear to the child, who not only hears it but also feels it: "You do not accept me for who I am and what I can do. You do not allow me to be authentic, genuine."

Unconditional love knows that it must put the dream aside and step in to help a child discover his own innate talents and abilities.

5. *Unconditional love allows consequences to occur.* By nature, most of us learn through experiences. It often takes the painful consequences of an action to make the lesson hit home.

A parent who desires to demonstrate acceptance of a child in a profound way may be required to step back and allow painful consequences to happen to the child. Unconditional love, quietly and often while hurting, stays in the shadows while circumstances develop growth in our children.

6. *Unconditional love is always there.* Children's bad choices—such as a surprise pregnancy or a drug-related problem—can stand like insurmountable walls against any hope of quality family relationships. Unconditional love, as it encompasses all the components discussed above, can withstand almost any situation that endangers the family's commitment to the promise. Unconditional love enables families to risk rejection, express feelings, squarely face reality, allow for authenticity, and remain bound together in the vows of the adoption promise.

THE ULTIMATE DIRECTION
FOR A POSITIVE, NURTURING ENVIRONMENT

Love is patient, love is kind, and is not jealous; love does not brag and is not arrogant, does not act unbecomingly; it does not seek its own, is not provoked, does not take into account a wrong suffered, does not rejoice in unrighteousness, but rejoices in the truth; bears all things, believes all things, hopes all things, endures all things. Love never fails.[7]

Creating a positive, nurturing family environment requires a knowledge of what all people, not just adopted children, need. When received, a child can grow and mature into a healthy adult. Those needs are:

■ To belong
■ To be authentic
■ To have a sense of dignity
■ To be valued
■ To be loved unconditionally

QUESTIONS FOR SMALL GROUPS
1. In what other ways can a sense of belonging be built into a child?
2. Why is establishing a sense of dignity so important for children adopted in older childhood?

3. What other ways can this be done?

4. Discuss the concept of unconditional love? Do you agree or disagree with the components listed?

CHAPTER TEN

What's Inside an Adopted Adolescent?

Helping Our Teens Resolve Five Painful Issues

By the time I was fourteen, I felt angry, alone, and left out.
All my friends knew their backgrounds, knew about their past.
They all knew where they were born. I didn't have one clue.
Everyone in my world kept me guessing.
Beth, age twenty-five, adopted as an infant

That Tuesday morning began just like any other for the Barkers. Ron and Melinda both left for work before their children were up.

The Barkers' two teenagers, Kathy (seventeen) and Mark (sixteen), had been adopted as infants. Kathy was just three weeks old. Mark, soon to follow, was just three days old when his family brought him home from the hospital.

Kathy grew into a beautiful young lady, tall and slender with curly brown hair. Because she was quiet and shy, she had just a small group of close friends. Dating intimidated her, so she was never available. She anxiously anticipated the end of the school year because school provided her with few positive encounters. Academically, it was tough. Socially, because she was so quiet, it was painful.

This year had been particularly tough for Kathy. She had withdrawn from even her small group of friends, spending a great deal of time alone in her room. For her parents, it was one battle after another just to get her to go to school each day.

Mark, in most respects, was quite the opposite. Shorter than his sister, with thick, blond hair, Mark was boisterous and somewhat sloppy. School wasn't a challenge for him; he earned excellent grades. Unlike his sister, Mark had a parade of friends who dropped by the house regularly. Phone calls from his peers usually disrupted the evening quiet.

Mark and Kathy were alike in only one way. Both struggled with growing-up issues that are unique to adopted teens, and both kept their distress in hiding. Kathy tucked her conflict away behind her quiet, compliant demeanor. Mark camouflaged his pain with noisy, "life of the party" behavior.

A FAMILY CRISIS

Melinda was meeting with her supervisor on Tuesday morning when a call from the high school counselor interrupted them.

"Where's Kathy this morning?" the voice inquired. "No one called to report an absence, and Mark says he doesn't have any idea where she is."

Puzzled, Melinda muffled an excuse and hung up. Immediately she called home. No answer. Explaining to her boss that she had a family emergency, Melinda rushed home.

Throughout the ten-minute drive to their home, Melinda kept telling herself that she was overreacting. "Don't worry—everything's fine," she reasoned. "Kathy's probably just running late."

Going in through the garage, Melinda walked into the family room. On the kitchen counter was a note:

> Mom and Dad,
> I have been so mixed up lately. I am so confused. I don't know who I am and what I am going to do with my life. I know that you've been concerned about me and that I've been a real problem lately. I thought if I just leave, then you won't have the problems anymore.

Melinda was dumbfounded. She had no idea that Kathy was struggling to that degree. She never dreamed in her wildest imagination that Kathy would run away. It was so unlike her. Melinda called Ron at work and asked him to come home right away.

BEGINNING WITH A PROMISE

As Melinda sat anxiously waiting for Ron to come, her thoughts sped back to the day when Kathy had entered their lives.

Five years into their marriage, Ron and Melinda had encountered a harsh reality — the realization that they would never conceive a child. Unexplained infertility stole their dreams. Determined to raise a family, however, they decided to adopt.

After months of waiting and then working through the lengthy homestudy, they had a glimmer of hope. The adoption agency called them about the possibility of adopting an infant girl. Within five days of that phone call, Kathy entered their lives. The Barkers began their adoption journey.

Six months after Kathy arrived, Melinda recalled, they stood before the judge to make a lifelong vow to her. They promised to love her, nurture her, and provide a permanent family for her. That promise was full of high expectations for themselves as parents. That promise was full of dreams for the child.

Up to this point, it seemed that their goals had been fulfilled. Yet beneath the surface lay a reservoir of untapped concerns.

The Barkers made their promise first to Kathy and then to Mark, with little or no understanding of the broader issues of adoption that confront every adoptive family. They did not know that buried within the adoptive relationship are special considerations unique to the adopted child. They did not realize that these questions surface most often as adopted children enter adolescence. They found out only when they crashed headlong into the difficulties their teenage daughter was facing.

WHAT IS AN ADOLESCENT?

Adolescents undergo the most dramatic period of change that they will experience in their lifetime. A twelve-year-old boy who began summer vacation short and stocky may return to school in the fall towering over many of his classmates.

In addition to incredible physical changes, adolescents go through turbulent mental and emotional transformations. They begin to see the world differently. As thinking processes deepen, they shift from the tangible preoccupations of middle childhood, in which they are focused only on things they can see or experience, to a view of life on a higher level.

Adolescents begin to ask profound questions such as "Who am I?" and "What am I going to do with my life?" and even, "What is the meaning of life?"

Adopted teens such as Kathy are no different from other adolescents. They struggle with the same questions. However, the weight of such complex issues is heavier. For as adopted adolescents struggle with life's normal transitions, they most often do so under the shadow of a history they do not fully understand.

Families facing problems in the adolescent years should examine two primary sources for the causes of those problems. First, before blaming the crisis on adoption, parents should take a look at what's happening within the family, at school, and in peer relationships. The household disruption might have nothing to do with adoption issues or past events; it could be related to current family functions, problems at school, or difficulties with friends. Second, after parents have examined current circumstances and dynamics, they should explore the issues to which adopted teens are particularly vulnerable. These concerns may provide additional clues to what's going on inside their teen's world.

WHAT'S HAPPENING INSIDE THE FAMILY?

A painful lesson that Jim and Melody Brochman learned was that their family communication lacked some essential skills in resolving conflicts.

The Brochmans' household, which included three adopted teenagers, was chronically conflictive. But the pervasive anger and frustration had more to do with how the family interacted with each other than it did with adoption-related concerns.

As Jim and Melody saw their home environment deteriorate into a war zone, they were courageous enough to seek help.

Melody commented about their situation:

> Counseling opened our eyes. I realized for the first time
> that when conflicts in the household arose, I always
> responded the same way. The kids would act up. I would
> begin yelling. Then I would become angry, and from fear
> of not knowing what to do, I would send the three children
> to their rooms.
>
> The result was twofold. First, conflicts remained
> unresolved. Second, my children got what they wanted—
> not having to take any responsibility for the problem.
>
> Both Jim and I are learning how to handle these situa-
> tions more effectively, be more assertive, and stick to pre-
> arranged house rules for all of us on how we deal with anger
> and problem solving. We are learning a better way.

Once families evaluate current home dynamics and the
whole environment of the adopted adolescent, they are ready to
learn about those issues that confront teens at their most vulnerable moments of development.

IDENTIFYING ADOPTED TEENS' MOST VULNERABLE ISSUES

The story of Kathy Barker is the story of a loving adoptive family
who thrived on the relationships they had developed with their
children. It is also the story of a family who was completely
unaware of the sensitive life issues that must be brought to
the surface for many adopted adolescents. Taking steps toward
resolving these issues as far as possible is necessary as the teen
separates from her adoptive family to form new relationships and
a new life as a young adult.

As mentioned earlier, adopted children gradually understand
the meaning of adoption on a developmental scale. By the time
the child reaches adolescence, she may perceive her adoption in
a far different light than what her parents believe she does. As
an adolescent, she is preoccupied not only with normal identity
struggles, but often with more unsettling questions such as "Who
am I really? Can I have a future if I don't know my whole past?

What is the truth about my separation from my birth family?"

As a result of the internal struggles, professionals and parents may note behavioral changes that go beyond the normal confrontation of issues in adolescence. These behavioral changes could be signals of a child's struggle with one or more of several primary adoption issues.[1]

In providing counseling to adopted adolescents, Dr. Alan Dupre-Clark, a clinical counselor, urges parents to define the primary issue with which the teen is struggling. Dr. Dupre-Clark describes this primary issue as "that one which provides the obvious handle on what the child is expressing about his birth origins through his behavior."[2] Once a primary issue is identified, then parents and counselors have much more insight with which to help their young person.

How does a parent recognize a child's main adoption issue? Primarily, by paying close attention to repeated behaviors. Teens are often not fully aware of what is happening within them. Their attitudes and behavior may be as confusing to themselves as they are to their parents.

ISSUE ONE: A CRY FOR CONTROL

Fran felt like slamming the phone receiver down, but she didn't. It was the high school principal again. Their fifteen-year-old son Steve was sitting in the office, suspended from class for the third time that month. This suspension meant he would be ineligible for the next three basketball games. *What has gotten into him?* she wondered. Steve's father had attempted to talk with him, but Steve just mumbled meaningless responses, so Mike decided to drop the subject.

Until this year, Steve hadn't experienced any major problems at home or at school. Of course, he'd had his share of detentions for minor infractions, but nothing as disruptive as what he was doing currently.

Steve had been a delightful youngster to raise—compliant, cooperative, and fun loving. He had become part of the Rossburg family at the age of three-and-a-half. His history painted a sad picture of extreme neglect and abuse, but Steve never seemed bothered by it. He generally did whatever was asked of him.

Struggling with confusion about her son's behavior, Fran made a decision. She called one of her friends, another adoptive mom of an adolescent, to ask her advice. After Fran described Steve's behavior, her friend suggested that perhaps Steve was calling out for some control in his life.

One common issue for adopted teens revolves around the need for control. Many feel that their lives have been overly managed or mismanaged by adults in their world. The mismanagement might have begun with their birth parents' decision to relinquish parental rights — or, even worse, their birth parents' loss of parental rights due to abuse or neglect.

Following that series of events, decisions were then made concerning future foster or adoptive parents, how much information would be available to them, and expectations regarding the child's behavior and acceptance of what life was handing to them. For some youngsters, years of frustrated feelings build up from their belief that they have had no control in their lives. A strong need to govern their own lives erupts in adolescence.

What Should Parents Look For?

The following behavioral signals may indicate that teens are struggling for a sense of control:

- More extreme limit-testing of authority figures
- Lying
- Behavior tantrums and verbal abuse of authority figures
- Breaking rules
- Chemical dependency
- Eating disorders
- Compulsive need to manage their world — extremely organized, always planning ahead

What Can Parents Do?

Teens struggling with lack of control can best move toward resolution as they are given more opportunities for choice, according to Betsy Keefer, co-consultant for the Parenthesis Post Adoption Project.[3] "Parents who can provide more opportunities for decision-making will discover that power struggles lessen in the home," says Keefer.

For example, within the framework of established boundaries, parents can give teens plenty of latitude in selecting clothes. For example, a youngster who is given a specific amount of money to spend on three pairs of pants, four shirts, and five pairs of socks will gain a sense of control in his life when he is allowed to choose his purchases.

Another opportunity for choice is the assignment of chores. Parents who work with Keefer in support groups are encouraged to offer the teen a number of options regarding what chores need to be completed, along with a time limit to complete those chores. Teens are reminded again of the variety of choices they have, but are also cued into the possibility of consequences should they not exercise those choices.

ISSUE TWO: REHEARSING REJECTION AND ABANDONMENT

"I can't imagine any kid being so bad that his parents dump him like a piece of trash."

"I'm not going to get too close to anyone—that way, I'll never be discarded again."

"My birth parents rejected me. When is this going to happen with my adoptive parents?"

"I have always had the fear that some morning I will wake up and nobody will be here. They will all have mysteriously disappeared."

Rejection ranks as one of life's most painful experiences. For some adopted children, especially in the vulnerable adolescent years, feelings of rejection and abandonment from their birth parents can override the positive and nurturing love of their adoptive family. Teens' perceptions of rejection can spill over to affect them in building healthy relationships. They can develop a pattern of pursuing acceptance and backing away from it when emotional intimacy appears close.

Robin, the beautiful sixteen-year-old daughter of Paul and Beth Clark, never dated a boy for very long. Robin was thrilled with the amount of attention she received from the young men in her school. She chatted enthusiastically with her mom about possible dating prospects. However, after a few dates, Robin invariably began refusing phone calls and rejecting further invitations. Her behavior stumped her parents.

Robin's confusing behavior is typical of a young person dealing with rejection issues. Robin was adopted by the Clarks at six weeks. Their openness about how she was separated from her family gave her information that was helpful to her. But she repeatedly asked two questions that the Clarks could not answer: "Why did they get rid of me? Why did they just leave me?" This theme of rejection was so strong with Robin that in most of her relationships, she rebuffed girlfriends and boyfriends before they rejected her.

What Should Parents Look For?

Characteristic behaviors in teens grappling with the perception of rejection and abandonment include the following:

- Successive cycles of pursuing friendships or relationships with abrupt termination of them; rejecting others before they can be rejected
- Negative behavior that sets up a pattern of perceived rejecting responses from adoptive family
- Expressing fear of being close to people
- In serious cases, depression and/or suicide attempts
- Resistance to the transition of teen to young adult
- Getting involved with the legal system
- Clinging, dependent behavior
- Truancy

What Can Parents Do?

Parents may find themselves totally unable to influence their teen's choice of friends. Keefer recommends that parents basically stay out of these affairs, instead concentrating on what message the child is receiving in the home. Remarkably, two-thirds of the families who come to the Parenthesis Post Adoption Project for support and intervention adopted their children as infants. Yet they still find that the issue of abandonment plays a very strong role in their children's lives.

Because the fear of rejection or abandonment can be so

strong, teens may set up the scenario to let it happen again. Volleying rejecting messages at adoptive parents such as "You're not my real dad" or "I don't want to be in the family" can easily pull a hurting, frustrated parent into returning similar rejecting messages. "If you don't stop this behavior, you are not going to be part of this family anymore," parents may retort.

To help a youngster deal with deep feelings of rejection and pain, Keefer suggests that parents monitor their responses to their teen's acting out. In heated moments parents have two choices: to respond in anger with rejecting remarks, or to remove themselves from the conflict momentarily in a kind of parental timeout. Most rejecting messages come in the midst of heated conflict.

Parents can also examine their own communication skills to determine what messages they are subtly or not-so-subtly sending to their children. Are they available to listen? Do they listen beyond the surface words? Are they able to ask questions that will get below the surface? Do they allow their teens to express feelings without judging them or reacting defensively? Good family communication sends a message that teens are accepted in their family.

Preteens and some older teens occasionally respond to the deep emotional scars of rejection and abandonment with changes in normal family living or in transitional periods of their lives.

If a parent becomes ill or plans a long trip, abandonment reactions may prompt negative behavior. These times require special awareness on the part of the parent and an effort to communicate about the teen's fears. Although youngsters in this age range understand cognitively that a parent will recover or return, they may stumble emotionally, says Keefer.

As teens move into the final year of high school, graduation may represent parental loss and perceived abandonment.

The fear of growing up and leaving home triggered an unconscious reaction in eighteen-year-old Brian, who attempted to sabotage the last semester of his senior year. Somewhere inside he was clinging to the thought, *If I don't graduate, my parents won't make me leave and go to college.*

One suggestion for parents sensing this type of reaction from their son or daughter is to plan their teen's departure from home in gradual steps. If teens plan to attend college or technical school, parents can suggest that they spend their first year living at home and commuting to a nearby school.

For young adults who are planning on working right after graduation, completing a plan for independent living may take up to two years.

ISSUE THREE: INVESTIGATING IDENTITY

A recurring comment made by adopted adolescents, especially in later years, is, "Who am I, *really?*" The identity crisis commonly attributed to the adolescent years is often compounded for adopted teens. Adoption experts give this the label "genealogical bewilderment." It is described as the "feeling of being cut off from your heritage, your religious background, your culture, your race."[4] Unlike their peers' usually thorough knowledge of their genetic roots and identification with a family, adopted children usually lack information about their beginning.

Dan's tremendous musical talent was the pride and joy of his musical parents. Just like his adoptive father, Dan could pick up a trumpet or sit at the piano and play superbly. Dan's confusion as he matured was, "Who am I really like—my birth family or my adoptive family?" Dan took on the characteristics of his adoptive parents. He knew what those were. He saw them every day. But what about the characteristics of his birth parents—were they musical? Was he more like them? He had no idea.

Casey, age seventeen, was nearing graduation and trying to decide what direction to take in her life. Casey knew the circumstances of her adoption. She was born to a teenage unwed mother who lived on welfare. Struggling with attempting to find some identity, Casey made some poor decisions. Just before graduation, she announced to her parents that she was pregnant. In spite of her parents' acceptance of the crisis and willingness to help, Casey moved out and into the apartment of her baby's father. She had chosen an identity on which to build her life. She was just like her birth mother.

What Should Parents Look For?

Teens grappling with identity generally signal their distress in one or more of the following ways:

- Easily giving in to peer or group pressure to be like others
- "Trying on" different identities, including those that they perceive might be characteristic of their birth parents
- Moody and brooding
- Clingy or manipulative with adults in their world
- Displaying a sense of helplessness
- Association with troubled peers

What Can Parents Do?

Keefer suggests that parents return to the agency that arranged the adoption and attempt to get as much information as possible. Even non-identifying information about birth parents that gives a physical description and interests can guide a child toward identity formation.

For parents in the early stages of the adoptive relationship and far from facing those adolescent years, Keefer recommends that they return to the agency to obtain similar information before the "trail gets cold. Get everything in writing so that the young person can read it for himself," she advises.

A second suggestion for helping a young person deal with identity issues is for parents to monitor how they feel and think about the child's birth parents. Adoptive parents occasionally feel threatened by the invisible presence of birth parents and may have a tendency to criticize them to the child.

"A child cannot feel good about himself until he feels good about where he came from," offered Keefer." Parents should be realistic and as positive as possible."

ISSUE FOUR: BEING ADOPTED IS DIFFERENT, AND IT FEELS THAT WAY

> Sometimes I look around the dinner table and think to myself, "I don't look like a single person here." There are times I feel like I really don't belong here. . . .
>
> I get so tired of people asking questions about my past . . . like, "Don't you want to meet your 'real' mom?"

or "Don't you ever wonder if you have brothers or sisters?" People sometimes are so insensitive and way too nosy. . . .

When we walk into a restaurant or grocery store, I feel people looking at us. I know they're wondering where my parents got me. I was born in Korea, and it is obvious that I'm adopted.

Many adopted adolescents remark that one issue following them through middle childhood into their teen years is feeling different. They may be keenly aware and sometimes ill at ease if their appearance is quite different from their adoptive family. This problem holds true especially for those adopted across racial or cultural boundaries. Some report that they feel somewhat disconnected from their family and the world they live in.

Not only is appearance a matter of difference, but, in rare cases, so is status in the family. "It always seemed like my younger brother, my parents' birth child, got all the breaks," remarked Amy, age nineteen. "My parents seemed harder on me. Maybe it was because I was older, or maybe it was because I was adopted. Anyway, I always felt different from him when it came to the relationship with our parents."

What Should Parents Look For?
Experiencing deep feelings of being different can create the following behavioral reactions in teens:

- Developing an offbeat or weird style of dress — "Since I feel different, I am going to look that way."
- Choosing an identity contrary to the adoptive family
- Devaluing themselves and seeking friendships with negative influences
- Chemical dependence, because the pain of being different is too difficult to cope with
- Chameleon-like behavior, in which circumstances and peers dictate behavioral identity — when they're with a drinking crowd, that's who they are; when they're with the church crowd, that's who they are
- Distancing intimacy in the home

What Can Parents Do?

To help a child with the issue of feeling different, parents can look outside their own family circle to other adoptive families. As they cultivate friendships with families in similar circumstances, their children will see others who are just like them.

Support groups provide a positive resource for families facing this need. More and more support organizations around the country are providing opportunities for adopted children to meet with each other through age-based groups and recreational activities.

ISSUE FIVE: A PART OF ME IS MISSING

"It's so difficult to describe how I feel. It's like a part of me isn't here. I feel empty."

Some adopted adolescents describe a feeling of being incomplete, empty, or like a vacuum inside. They credit that perception to the lack of birth family ties in the loss of their birth parents. They also say that they have been unable to fill that void with a substitute, no matter how loving and nurturing that person has been. For some adopted kids, the feeling of emptiness is so strong that it causes them to turn inward and blocks their ability to give and receive love.

What Should Parents Look For?

A deep sense of emptiness or incompleteness can result in serious behavioral problems. Some parents have reported the following struggles with their middle-to-late adolescent child:

- Chemical dependence
- Depression and multiple suicide attempts
- Attempted, successful, and recurrent pregnancies
- Overeating or anorexia
- Seeking mother figures

What Can Parents Do?

According to Keefer, this issue of emptiness is perhaps the most serious of all adolescent issues, and it can best be resolved by attempting to remove a portion of the child's source of grief — the loss of birth parents.

How is this accomplished? In some cases, adoptive parents have been able to secure a letter or video from a birth family member. They have contacted the agency that acted as a liaison between the adoptive family and the birth family. In some extreme cases, where the grief has created very serious, even life-threatening, adjustment problems, a possible reunion between the child and his or her birth family may alleviate the pain.

Adoptive families generally have many concerns about attempting such a drastic measure for their teenage child, such as: How will this affect my child? How will this reunion affect our relationship? However, for a child and family bordering on a life-threatening crisis or torn apart by drug or alcohol abuse, there isn't much to lose.

This was the case for seventeen-year-old Andrea Mitchell. In her preteen years, Andrea showed little interest in the whole subject of adoption. She knew that she had entered her family at birth directly from the hospital. She had been informed of her circumstances, and her parents were readily available to answer any questions she might have. She had grown up in a loving family. She knew she was their pride and joy.

However, as she neared her middle teen years, Andrea began to ask more penetrating questions. Her parents noticed a dramatic change in their sensitive child's behavior. She became increasingly depressed and withdrawn. Attempts at getting her to talk were unsuccessful. Andrea just didn't know what was the matter.

Andrea's problem hit a crisis level. One morning when Andrea failed to get out of bed for school, her mother, Cynthia, knocked on her door. When there was no answer, she cracked the door open to find her daughter apparently still asleep. As she walked over to awaken her, her foot crushed a pill bottle on the floor near the bed. Attempts to rouse Andrea failed. Cynthia rushed out to call for emergency help and then for her husband, Peter, at work.

Fortunately for Andrea and her family, her suicide attempt was unsuccessful. Following her recovery, the entire family entered therapy. The theme that consistently recurred from Andrea was, "There's this feeling inside, like a huge, gaping hole that always has been there. It just doesn't go away. It feels like a part of me is missing. I just got so tired of feeling that way."

One strong recommendation from the therapist for the Mitchell family, which the entire family was willing to pursue, was to initiate a search for Andrea's birth family. Her parents contacted a regional organization that specialized in such undertakings. Their questioning brought to mind some old information that Peter Mitchell had long stored away.

Two months prior to Andrea's birth, when the Mitchells were sitting in their attorney's office, an apparently unrelated phone call interrupted their meeting. Following the conversation, the lawyer wrote down the name of a Patricia Smith and her expected due date. The information caught Peter's eye. On impulse he made a mental note of the name and the woman's due date, and later placed it on a piece of paper in Andrea's adoption file at home.

When Peter went to that old file at the suggestion of the search group, he pulled out the note he had kept. The woman's due date was within five days of Andrea's birth. Perhaps this was a lead.

Following a four-month search, Andrea's birth mother was located just an hour's drive from the Mitchells. She agreed to a meeting, and the family met her in a park in their area. Since that day, Andrea keeps in contact with her birth mother sporadically. She doesn't intend to establish a close relationship with her at this point in her life. In her words,

> The Mitchells are my parents. They have loved me and cared for me. Meeting Patricia was the most important thing I could have done, for it enabled me to close the book on the past I never knew. It filled in an incredible sense of emptiness that was gnawing away at me. I feel complete and whole.

Let me offer a suggestion of caution for families taking this step: First, work through the entire process with a counselor who is sensitive to these types of issues. Because, second, there are possible circumstances that may block contact with birth parents—either they cannot be found or refuse to have contact or become reinvolved in the child's life.

"MY PARENTS HAVE DONE SO MUCH FOR ME"

On the bright side of the issues confronting teens during the upheaval of their adolescent years is the common theme of gratitude. Their words say it best.

Anna, age nineteen (adopted at three months)

I know how important I am to my parents. All throughout my growing up they told me in so many ways.

One of the hardest things I struggled with was going to them and asking for information about my birth parents. Their response was overwhelmingly positive. I know it came from a heart that felt some pain, like I would reject them or something. But they helped me in spite of their concern. Their response was born out of sensitivity to me and my needs. I am deeply grateful for the home in which I grew up.

Richard, age twenty (adopted at five)

I don't remember a whole lot about coming to my family. What I do remember were the problems that erupted when I was in late elementary school and junior high. I was some mixed-up kid. Late at night, after I had gone to bed, I would hear my parents talking about me while sitting in the kitchen. I heard such words as, "Richard has so much to offer. He is a talented young boy. With help, I know we will see him through this. Our family will make it." I never heard words that gave me any idea that they were ready to dump me.

I can't express enough how much I love my parents and hope someday I can repay them. I know when times get tough for them, I'll stick right by them.

Kimberly, age eighteen (adopted from Korea at five months)

The most meaningful experience I have had with my parents was the trip we took to Korea when I was fifteen. They had always been so open about my special issues—cultural things like that.

Although we couldn't locate any specific information about

my birth family, I was able to see how they would have lived and what it would have been like for me. Our trip there provided me with much more information. However, it gave me something else. It deeply impressed upon me how much my parents love me. I hope someday they will truly know how very much I am grateful to them for all they have been to me.

AN EPILOGUE

On the evening of Kathy Barker's disappearance, she called her parents from a friend's home in another town. She had walked down that morning to the bus station and caught a bus to her friend's town. Crying, she told them that she felt so mixed up and lost. She wanted to get help.

Ron and Melinda were deeply relieved after Kathy's call. The following week, the Barkers made an appointment with a counselor in their area who specialized in adoption-related issues.

Following almost six months of family counseling, the Barkers have stronger relationships today. They now are more aware that their children, a special miracle in their lives, will have issues that other teens will not. They also learned that the issues may possibly surface and resurface during transitional phases of their children's adult lives. They know that Kathy and Mark will still need their adoptive parents for support—because adoption is not one isolated event: it is a relationship that begins, grows, and is sustained by a lifelong promise.

> Each of us has things to which we return now and then to work on and worry over—things from the past and present that occasionally resurface. . . . It may be a relationship to a sister, it may be a fear of flying, it may be a tragic first love affair. . . . We tuck these issues away in a hatbox, in a closet, in a far-off corner of the house.
>
> Every now and then, something makes us search out that far-off corner, open the closet door, take down the box, and deal with the issue for a while. Eventually, we feel finished with it, at least for the time being, so we put

away the box and go back to living our lives. Some day in the future, though, we'll go back to that closet again, and deal with the issue in the box for a while longer.

That's what the adoption issue is like for most adoptees — no more, no less.[5]

SUMMARY

Some adopted adolescents walk through their teen years giving little thought to the issues surrounding their adoption experience. For others, those issues begin to block emotional development, affect relationships, and threaten self-esteem.

It is important for adoptive parents to know the potential issues that may confront their teens and understand how to deal with them should they arise. It is also crucial for these same families to evaluate how their own family dynamics may be affecting their children.

Five key issues that may confront adopted teens include:

■ A cry for control
■ Rehearsing rejection and abandonment
■ Investigating identity
■ Being adopted is different, and it feels that way
■ A part of me is missing — emptiness

QUESTIONS FOR SMALL GROUPS

1. What issues do you feel are confronting the teen in your home?

2. What behaviors have you found confusing or even disturbing?

3. What steps have you taken, if any, to work on these issues?

4. What have you found to be valuable in helping your teen?

CHAPTER ELEVEN

Transcultural Adoption:
Preparing for Special Challenges

Our adoption changed the character of our family forever.
We are not a Caucasian family who has adopted a minority child.
We are a minority family. We will always be.
An adoptive father

Transracial adoption: A child adopted by a family of a different race.
Intercountry adoption: A child from one culture adopted
by a family of another.
Transcultural adoption: A blending of both.

C radling a bright yellow blanket, Patsy Royer scooted out the car door and stepped to the sidewalk. Scott, her husband, hurriedly parked the car and walked briskly to met Patsy at the airport terminal door. In just an hour, a plane would land that carried within it all their hopes and dreams for a family. Inside that plane rode their newly adopted five-month-old Korean daughter.

Joy Meyer, their caseworker, met them in front of the ticket counter as planned.

"Here's the blanket you asked me to bring," Patsy offered. "In all the excitement, I didn't ask you what it was for."

"It has a very special purpose," Joy replied. "When I board the plane to identify your daughter, I will have her escort wrap her in this blanket. Because all passengers deplane and go straight through customs, it will take a long time. If you watch the line, you will see that colorful blanket. Then you will know that she is here for sure!" Joy reassured them.

That is exactly what happened for this excited couple. As the passengers walked through customs, that yellow blanket stood out in the crowd. The Royers' waiting was over. Emily Ann was home!

When a family makes the decision to adopt across racial or cultural lines, whether that family is European-American, African-American, Hispanic-American, or of some other ethnic origin, they are making a decision to alter the course not only of their generation but of generations to come. They are no longer a family of one race or culture. They become a multicultural, multiracial, multiethnic family — forever. They can expect both praise and prejudice from the society in which they live.

How can families best prepare for the joys, challenges, and realities of such a decision? How can these families prepare their children to live successfully in society as minority members of that society? These critical questions deserve careful examination.

FAMILIES CAN PREPARE
BY EXAMINING THEIR MOTIVATION

What inspires a family to pursue transracial or transcultural adoption has been the subject of multiple studies. The majority of these studies noted that most parents are motivated by concern for children for whom it is difficult to find adoptive families. In another examination, the recurrent theme for adopting transracially was "compassion for children without homes."[1] Still others report that their decision was motivated by their understanding of God's direction in their lives.

"It just seemed that doors opened widely for us, guiding us toward transcultural adoption," commented one adoptive father. "After we saw Jacob's picture, of course we were excited. But the feeling was deeper than that. It was like this is supposed to be."

Families state many positive reasons for pursuing transcultural adoption. However, because most transcultural adoptions occur within the European-American community, Pamela Severs, an independent Children Services consultant, cites three reasons she has observed that could lead to fractured promises.

WE COULDN'T GET A CAUCASIAN CHILD

Dennis and Cheri Jennings are childless. They know that it is virtually impossible for them to adopt a healthy, white infant. So they asked to be put on the waiting list to adopt a biracial infant. In a moment of honest examination, Dennis commented, "Our first choice is to find a baby of our same race, but we know that will never, never happen. A baby's a baby, isn't it? We said we would take a mixed-race child."

This type of parental attitude—bargaining for a second choice—is a troubling one, according to Severs. It can lead to difficulties in the relationship down the road when the family faces racial or cultural pressures.

"During the sixties and seventies, I think a lot of white couples were looking at biracial (black/white) as an alternative," says Severs. "Some of the thinking at that time was, 'we can't get a white child, so we will get at least a half-white. We will push aside the black issue. We will raise this child as part of the Caucasian world.' This is a dangerous, explosive road on which to journey."[2] It sends a message to the child that, in reality, his family denies who he really is.

Ellie's story illustrates a family's failure to recognize the differences inherent in transcultural adoption and to communicate with a child about the value in those differences.

Ellie, age five, came down with a bad case of poison ivy. Concerned, her mother took her to the doctor. After her appointment, Ellie came strutting out of the doctor's office, pulling on her eyelids to make them slanted.

"Dr. Young sure had funny-looking eyes," Ellie laughed.

Pam stopped on the sidewalk. She was dumbfounded. A thought hit her abruptly. For the first time, she realized that apparently Ellie had no concept of herself. Ellie's appearance was similar to that of her Asian doctor, for Ellie was from Hong Kong. Surely Ellie knew she was different, but she had never been given a way of understanding it or talking about it.

Families pursue transcultural adoptions not only because a white child is unable to be located, but also because they genuinely love to parent. On the surface, that is an honorable motive. But there is a flip side.

WE ARE COLORBLIND

"Some people are just natural parents," Severs remarks." They really love children. They really love to parent. What concerns me as a negative is that they are colorblind. They do not see a black child. They do not see an Asian child. They do not see a Hispanic child. They think that color or race doesn't matter. They parent the child with the philosophy that love is enough." Love is crucial, but an element of love is reality. "Race *does* make a difference," asserts Severs. "It is who we are."[3]

Two questions asked by workers selecting families for transcultural adoptions are crucial: "Can a family with this perspective ever truly give their minority child the skills to survive in this world? Can they learn that love *isn't* enough?"

Adoptive parents who freely and openly recognize the child's differences will have the energy and motivation to deal with general parenting demands and also with pressures from a community that may not deal empathically with interracial adoptions.

A third reason for transcultural adoption also spells potential relationship difficulties.

WE ARE GOING TO INTEGRATE THIS WORLD

Some parents step into the arena of transcultural adoption with a singular purpose—to make some type of social statement. The adoption is their altruistic way of solving part of society's complex problems. This kind of adoption is not about a child. It is about a crusade.

A family motivated primarily by a cause will soon find the fervor of the crusade diminished by reality. If the family hasn't moved past their primary motivation and into a realistic and nurturing relationship with the child, they have created a disaster waiting to happen.

As families examine their motives for transcultural adoption, they can also prepare by assessing their own readiness.

FAMILIES CAN PREPARE BY ASSESSING THEIR READINESS

Before the homestudy is completed, families are already anxiously anticipating the arrival of a child. Getting ready for the newest family member requires significant preparation, emotionally and educationally.

"Learn as much as you can about the culture of your child before he comes," advises Jeanette Casey, adoptive mom of a Korean child. "I mean much more than just foods and dress. Learn how people relate to each other. Even infants."

When five-month-old Whitney joined Jeanette, her husband Dave, and their children, they were not aware of an important part of Korean interaction: Korean children are not taught to make direct eye contact. Whitney's early months were spent in a culture in which she never experienced consistent, regular eye contact. When she arrived home, she would not look at her new parents. It concerned them initially. "After a few days, she gradually began to look at us. It took time, but she eventually connected," Jeanette said. Had they known that small piece of information, their initial concerns would not have come up.

When Mick and Liz McAllister, parents of two Korean youngsters, contemplated intercountry adoption, they took a long look at the future. "We tried to be realistic. Would our children be accepted in this community? Would there be enough activities and opportunities for them to be with other Asian children? We had to look at those long-term issues. We will have these cute little babies, but they will grow up. They will go to school here. They will eventually want to date."

Their assessment brought positive results. Although they lived in a rural area, there was an outstanding plus.

"We have a college in our community with a good number of international students," Liz said. "We also live in an integrated neighborhood because of the school. There are Filipino and Indian children. This neighborhood has remained stable. We knew we would be living here for quite a while."

In the midst of excitedly anticipating the arrival of their biracial children, Jeff and Kim Franklin knew that they would be taking on the responsibility for providing a lifestyle in which their children would be able to absorb the African-American culture. The first step they took was to move from their secluded, suburban neighborhood into a fully integrated neighborhood. The second step was to locate an integrated church where they would be fully embraced and loved.

In an effort to help families prepare for transcultural adoption, the following self-assessment guide offers in-depth questions a family can examine in the early stages of the process.

❖ ❖ ❖

AM I READY TO ADOPT TRANSCULTURALLY?
A Self-Assessment Guide for Prospective Adoptive Parents
By Pamela Severs[4]

Please take time to discuss these issues with your family. Also, remember that there is not always a clear right and wrong answer. These topics are meant to encourage discussion, openness, and honesty.

Your Own Cultural Identity and Knowledge of Other Cultures
- When and how did you first become aware of your race and ethnicity?
- What role has this played in forming your values and attitudes?
- What is your earliest memory of a person of another race?
- What do you know about the race and culture of the child you want to adopt?
- How personally involved are you with other races and cultures?
- Have you had experience as a minority person? If so, what were your feelings?
- Can you identify positive role models in the culture of the child you wish to parent?
- What are the similarities and differences between your culture and the culture of your child?
- How can you begin to establish racial identity for an infant? For an older child?

Your Support for Transcultural Adoption
- What led you to consider transcultural adoption?
- Do you know other parents who have already adopted

transculturally?
- Are there people of other cultures or races within your immediate or extended family?
- Have you discussed transcultural adoption with the significant people in your life? With friends and neighbors who will be part of your future support system?
- How have others reacted to your adoption of a child of a different race or culture? Are you prepared to communicate comfortably and knowledgably with others as needed?

Opportunities for Cultural and Racial Awareness
- What is the racial composition of your neighborhood, school, and church?
- Will your child usually be "the different one" at family and social functions?
- Can you identify attitudes in your community concerning the child's culture and race?
- Are same-race role models and peers available to the child on a daily basis?
- What racially mixed functions do you attend?
- Are you comfortable around others who are of a different race?

Your Parenting Skills
- What do you already know about the child's dietary, skin, hair, and health care needs?
- Where can you go to learn about the personal care of the child?
- How will you teach the child about his or her own culture and race?
- How will you involve same-race people in the child's life?
- How do you think transcultural adoption may have a negative effect on you? On your family?
- How will you respond to the child when he or she is called racially derogatory names?

■ How do you think the child will feel about growing up in a family of a different race or culture?

❖ ❖ ❖

Families can best prepare for the joys and challenges of trans-cultural parenting by examining their motives and assessing their own attitudes and those of their extended family, friends, and community.

HOW FAMILIES CAN PREPARE THEIR CHILDREN FOR LIFE AS ETHNIC MINORITY MEMBERS OF SOCIETY

Following the question of how families can prepare themselves is a second question: "How can these families prepare their child to live successfully in society as a minority member of that society?" This challenge can be answered by exploring three specific issues: (1) How early in life does a child form racial identity? (2) How can the child's cultural heritage be maintained? (3) What method can parents use to help their child deal with prejudicial comments?

RACIAL AWARENESS AND IDENTITY DEVELOP EARLY

"Hey, Patrick, open your eyes so you can see," laughed Shane, Patrick's five-year-old playmate. On sunny days, when five-year-old Korean-born Patrick plays outside, he squints to block the sun. It looks like he walks around with his eyes closed. His friend's innocent comment only reminded Patrick yet again that he was different.

Awareness of differences begins early in a child's life, especially in the area of racial awareness. A three-year-old is aware of people's color difference. By four, a child understands that these color differences have racial implications that place people into specific groups.[5]

Differentiation continues in the growing child. By the age of five, a child has formed attitudes about those differences.[6]

Where do these attitudes emerge from? Parents generally do not teach children directly about the positive or negative side of racial differences. Children develop their thinking by observing and absorbing the attitudes of adults in their world. These same children then transmit their attitudes to children of other races with whom they have daily contact.

How can parents best help their child to develop a positive racial identity? Primarily, by helping him or her form a well-rounded, positive self-concept and develop self-esteem. Dr. David Brodzinsky defines self-concept as how children see themselves. He describes self-esteem as how much they like what they see.[7]

"Parents should make sure, without going overboard, that they recognize the differences and communicate the values of those differences to the child," commented Jeanette Casey. "When Whitney struggles with being different from us or her friends, we listen to her feelings. Then we highlight something of her beautiful Korean features. Whitney also participates in a play group for Korean children. This is essential. We feel that she needs to see other kids just like her with white parents," Jeanette concluded.

This family, like hundreds of other transcultural families, has learned that the development of their child's self-esteem and self-concept is intrinsically tied to building a racial and ethnic connection.

A child must have help in developing a strong sense of racial identity. Parents can accomplish this through using two resources: a "cultural consultant" and a "cultural heritage plan." Both of these concepts were developed by Pamela Severs.

The Cultural Consultant
Parents who have never experienced the difficulties inherent in living as an ethnic minority member of a society comment that they have little or no concept of what it feels like. These parents may make tremendous efforts to learn about the culture of their child through literature, networking with other adoptive parents, and opening themselves up to a diversity of cultural and racial experiences. However, they may still feel unable to fully identify with their child.

Some parents have found a very helpful way to make an empathic connection across racial boundaries: forming a trusting relationship with an individual who is of the same race and culture as their child. Pamela Severs calls this individual a "cultural consultant."

Juan came to the United States as an exchange student from Central America in the mid-eighties. During an international dinner hosted on his college campus, he met Andy and Connie Parker, parents of three Guatemalan children.

During his four years as a student, Juan developed a warm friendship with the Parkers. They sought his guidance in handling negative racial attitudes and issues that confronted the children when they entered school. They sought his advice on specific dietary, skin, and health care from a cultural perspective. Juan also functioned as a resource for specific cultural foods, dress, holidays, and customs so that the Parkers could celebrate their children's heritage. He helped to educate them on the coping skills that the children would need to combat racism. Most importantly, Juan listened to them and encouraged them as they created an environment where their children would value their culture and, more importantly, themselves.

Although Juan is now half a world away, the family still maintains regular contact with him. He has become an invaluable, lifelong friend to them.

A cultural consultant is a valuable resource for a family in rearing their child whose ethnic origin is different from their own. Additionally, the development of a "cultural heritage plan" is a helpful companion in the effort to maintain the child's racial or cultural roots. Even families with young children can begin this process. The following plan lists suggested activities for families with children from infancy to middle adolescence.

❖ ❖ ❖

THE CULTURAL HERITAGE PLAN
By Pamela Severs[8]

Infancy: Birth to Eighteen Months
1. Establish the cultural consultant relationship.
2. Expose the infant to caretakers of different skin colors, different voice and language patterns, and different smells.

3. Provide various types of instrumental and vocal music that are culturally mixed.

Preschool: Two to Five Years

1. Continue the development of adult and child relationships with individuals of the child's racial and cultural origin.
2. Establish same-race role models both in fiction and real life.
3. Utilize same-race services and community providers such as doctors, baby-sitters, etc.
4. Provide culturally appropriate dolls, musical instruments, puzzles, picture books, and stories.
5. Assure that the child is provided with same-race contacts at church, in the neighborhood, or at day care and nursery school.

School Age: Six to Nine Years

1. Continue to develop same-race adult and child relationships.
2. Introduce culturally appropriate magazines, holiday celebrations, flags, maps, history, religion, and language tapes.
3. Make an assessment of the child's potential strengths, talents, and skills and expose the child to whatever opportunities will enhance those skills (for example, music lessons, sports, dancing, art class).
4. Establish support systems with veteran families who have adopted transculturally, and include the child in as much of that support as possible in picnics, outings, parties, etc.
5. Make a "like" statement to the child every day. "You laugh like your daddy. You swim like your brother."

Preadolescence: Ten to Twelve Years

1. Continue to maintain culturally appropriate dress, music, literature, associations, and art within the home.
2. Increase involvement with groups and social networks

of the same race and culture as the child that include *all* family members.
3. Create with the child a "History of the (African-American/Native American/Hispanic-American/Asian-American) People" scrapbook. Collect any newspaper articles, photos, and cards that depict racial and cultural achievements specific to the child's origin.

Early Adolescence: Thirteen to Fourteen Years
1. "Circle the wagons" by ensuring that the child is provided with consistent rules and expectations within the family unit.
2. Increase involvement with veteran families and the cultural consultant to differentiate normal adolescent behavior from cultural, racial, and adoptive issues.
3. Conduct regular, "no excuse for absence" family meetings.
4. While continuing the "History of . . ." scrapbook, encourage the child to develop his or her own plan for cultural and racial preservation in adulthood. Utilize this time to explore issues of dating, sexuality, marriage, and children in a non-threatening setting.
5. Provide ample and repeated opportunity for the child to discuss racial identity with outside professionals such as agency staff, psychologists, teachers, ministers, coaches, and veteran families.

Middle Adolescence: Fifteen to Seventeen Years
1. Reintroduce and encourage the development of same-race adult role models for the young person. Recognize that the young person may only accept those individuals with whom he has identified himself.
2. Continue the young person's involvement in her own plan for cultural and racial preservation.
3. "Claim" the young person's future role in the family, such as "We'll probably spoil our grandchildren," or "We're putting you in charge of the Christmas tree from now on."

4. Maintain involvement in culturally appropriate activities without the young person to demonstrate the long-term commitment of cultural preservation from the entire family.

5. Build upon the previously established cultural and racial lifestyle by presenting "family heirlooms" to the young person that have been established as culturally significant for him or her.

❖ ❖ ❖

Establishing a relationship with an adult of the same racial and cultural origin as the adopted child will provide tremendous insight for parents. As the child grows, following the steps of the cultural heritage plan will reap lifelong benefits. Finally, helping the child develop a plan to handle hurting and cutting remarks throughout life is one more effort that parents can employ to guide their child toward successful living.

HELPING A CHILD TO DEVELOP A PLAN FOR COPING WITH TEASING AND INSULTS

"Hey, Chinese eyes, who said you could ride this bus?"

"Go home, kid. Only white kids can play on this playground."

Entering elementary school for some minority youngsters can abruptly throw them into the reality of a world that may not be as friendly and warm as the safe, happy home environment they have enjoyed. In some areas of the country, racial prejudice runs strong and definitely filters down into the school-age population.

Helping a child develop coping strategies for dealing with insensitive racially or culturally motivated remarks, or simply to handle curious questions from others, is a critical task for parents. The need for these strategies begins as soon as the child walks in the front door of the kindergarten room – or earlier. If these skills are learned in the early years, the young adult adoptee will be well prepared for the task of entering society with confidence.

Most parents readily feel their child's emotional pain when

remarks slam against the child's vulnerable feelings. However, if they don't know how to manage such behavior from the outside, they might tend to minimize it.

"Oh, I'm sure that Christopher didn't really mean that," one parent might say, hoping to defuse the situation. However easy this approach may be, it does not deal with the child's pain.

When a child comes home reporting a painful incident or a barrage of questions at school, church, or in the neighborhood, parents can teach the child to manage those situations with the following steps.

1. *As a parent, don't overreact.* Don't run to the phone or out the door to confront the offender.

2. *Ask the child to explain exactly what happened.*

3. *Encourage the child to tell you how it felt to him.* Have him use descriptive terms such as "I felt angry, I felt scared, I felt sad, I felt lonely, I felt rejected."

4. *Ask your child, "What did you say or do when this happened? How did you handle it?"*

5. *Ask the child, "How do you think you might handle it differently in the future?"* Communicate to the child that he has choices. If he has trouble coming up with possible options, offer some alternatives.

Parents can give their child his best handle for coping with invading questions by equipping him with a cover story about his background.[9] To develop such a tool, the following suggestions may be helpful:

1. *Determine the questions people may ask and situations the child may encounter.* For example: imagine introducing the child to the neighborhood children; picture the child's first school day and the questions the teacher may ask; project what would happen when moving into a new neighborhood or joining a new church or community organization.

2. *Establish what information should be shared.* Children have difficulty sorting out what should be shared and what should be kept private. To help them resolve this dilemma, they can be instructed to provide three basic responses to questions. The three replies most often needed are the child's name, origin, and circumstances of adoption.

Should a person probe more intensely about the child's origin, the youngster can reply simply by giving the name of the city or state and following it with a question: "Where do you come from?" If a questioner wants to know why the child is where he is, youngsters can answer briefly without a lot of details. If the questioner persists, the child can learn to respond, "That's our family business. My family will have to answer that."

One very important thing for a child to know is that he is not obligated to tell everyone his life story: He has personal boundaries others should learn to respect. He can't choose how people in his world will react to him, but he can learn skills for choosing his own assertive response.

3. *Ask the child, "Is there anything you want me to do about this incident?"* Although children do not usually want direct parental involvement, it will help them feel secure to know the possibility exists.[10]

As children are given the opportunity to express the circumstances of the offense, to deal with their corresponding feelings, and to recognize the choices they have for responding, they will develop a growing understanding of how to handle insensitive people. The skills will serve them throughout life.

Parents can't shield their minority children from the possible onslaught of racial prejudice. They can only walk through the crisis with them. In the early years, they can equip their children with a healthy sense of belonging, personal and racial identity, and cultural connections. They can provide a family environment where the parents model recognition and acceptance of racial differences. Finally, they can create a setting where the regular flow of minority children and their families in and out of the home is a natural part of who they all are—a transcultural family.

SUMMARY

Parents who choose to adopt a child across racial or cultural boundaries elect to alter their family's structure for generations to come. Before making such a decision, families can prepare by evaluating their motivation for the adoption and assessing their readiness for the consequences it will entail.

After the child has entered the family, two significant resources can aid the family in maintaining the child's cultural ties: the cultural consultant and the cultural heritage plan.

QUESTIONS FOR SMALL GROUPS

1. Which of the assessment questions, if any, were particularly difficult for you? Why?

2. What is your motivation for pursuing transcultural adoption?

3. What are the attitudes of your extended family, your church, and your community?

4. Do you feel that a family who is unable or unwilling to initiate at least a portion of the cultural heritage plan should not consider an adoption of this type? Why, or why not?

5. What other benefits do you see in enlisting the help of a cultural consultant?

CHAPTER TWELVE

Searching for a Past:
Why Adopted Children Seek Their Roots and How Parents Can Respond

The letter was fragile and yellowed with age.
It was written by my birth mother at the time I was born. She was only sixteen.
The letter expressed love and concern for me. For the first time in my life,
I felt worthy of love. I knew my adoptive parents loved me,
but I never felt worthy of it.
Marcia, age thirty-two

R andy hesitated on the cracked sidewalk bordering the front yard. Then she stepped carefully through the litter-cluttered lawn and climbed the uneven steps to the door. She was apprehensive, scared. Did she really want to go in? It was hard to believe this day had come. All her life she had tucked away questions about her birth parents. Today, she would finally get some answers.

Randy had been only four years old when she and her older sister walked out the door of an orphanage hand in hand with two strangers. Those two strangers were to be her new mother and father. The children were given no further explanations. They just left.

By the time she was five, her parents had finalized her adoption. Like many people, Randy's parents believed that when a child is adopted at such a young age, the door is shut on the past. Some assume that all issues surrounding a child's earlier life are erased, and the youngster enters the new family with a blank slate.

However, like many adopted children, Randy's experience brought only a lifetime of questions. "Why did my birth parents leave me? Do I have other sisters and brothers? Who do I look like?" These questions gnawed away at her feeling of well-being, attacking sensitive and deep issues in self-esteem and personal identity. She felt robbed of a sense of belonging.

"Although I knew my adoptive parents loved me," she said, "I felt that pieces of my life were scattered and no one knew where they were. I had to find them."

WHY ADOPTED CHILDREN SEARCH FOR THEIR ROOTS

Randy's yearning to find a connection to her birth family's history is not an unusual occurrence for adopted children. Activating a hunt for one's origin and history can be motivated by many reasons, ranging from a need for medical and genealogical information to a deep, innate craving to unite with family ties from the past.

Chuck excelled in high school and earned a four-year science scholarship to a well-known university. He dreamed of one day pursuing a career as a medical missionary. He never really thought about tracking down information about his birth parents. When a crisis hit, however, it became a necessity.

Over the course of his junior winter semester, Chuck noticed a dramatic deterioration in his vision. He immediately sought the care of a specialist, who told him that his problem was potentially critical and most likely genetic in nature. At that point, some answers about Chuck's genetic heritage were imperative. He began the search only for genealogical and medical information. He was not interested in developing a relationship with his birth family.

Chuck's hurried and dramatic investigation brought heart-wrenching results. Although he never wanted or obtained specific information identifying his birth parents, he did obtain medical records revealing a history of blindness on his father's side. His father had been completely blind by age thirty. The report Chuck obtained offered him some hope, however, because it enabled his physician to offer potentially preventive treatment.

Shelly initiated her research for an entirely different reason. By the time she turned twenty-five, both of her adoptive parents had died, leaving only Shelly and her younger sister. She had never taken the opportunity to make inquiries about her past out of concern that her parents would misunderstand. Spurred on by a yearning to connect to her roots and a hunger for a parental relationship, Shelly began attempting to locate her birth family so that she would at least have some family ties. She has not yet located her birth parents, but she did discover two sisters who were adopted prior to her birth. All live within the same state.

Chuck's need for medical information and Shelly's desire to find a family she could belong to are just two reasons for a birth search. Adoption experts and adopted adults cite even more specific issues that initiate the walk into the past.

PARENTS DON'T COMMUNICATE

One primary factor that activates the search is dissatisfaction with the adoptive parents' communication.[1]

Jenny was adopted in 1963 as a two-year-old. She remembers being told of her adoption status perhaps twice prior to adolescence:

No one ever mentioned the word *adoption* around me, so I couldn't ask anyone about it. In the sixties people just didn't talk about it, like it was a horrible secret. By late elementary school, I knew I was different and adoption wasn't normal. I began wondering then, was it bad?

Parents choose to deal with adoption communication from a wide continuum of options. Some parents desire to keep the matter a closed subject, virtually denying its reality. These parents have adopted the coping style of rejection of differences (see chapter 7).

In contrast, other families communicate openly and honestly about the details of the entire adoption experience. In this acknowledgment of differences coping style, parents allow themselves and the child to explore the many facets of adoption.

They are open with the information they have concerning the child's life. They accumulate adoption-related books and other literature and make it accessible to the child.

The trend toward openness in relating information to the adopted child seems to lessen some trauma and stress related to his or her experiences. One specialist reported, "From our experience, we have learned that many psychological problems are directly related to secrecy or anonymity. We are convinced that the closed system must be replaced with . . . openness and honesty."[2] Finding out the whole story is one compelling factor in tracing the past. Finding someone for identifying family resemblance is another.

WHOM DO I LOOK LIKE? WHOM DO I ACT LIKE?

When Penny, a thirty-year-old with auburn hair and freckles, opened a manila envelope from the adoption agency, she certainly didn't expect to find what she did. The contents ended a lifetime of wondering, "Do I look and act like anyone in my family history?"

Dear Ms. Wright,

I am enclosing the social/medical information that you requested. We have the following non-identifying information concerning your birth family:

Social and Medical History of Penny Carter Wright

Father: Your birth father was a single, white, Protestant young man and was twenty-one years old at the time of your birth. He had dark hair, green eyes, and a medium complexion. He stood five-foot-nine and weighed 160 at the time of your birth. He was described by close friends as quiet and reserved. He shared many of the same interests as your mother. He enjoyed art and music and played both the piano and the guitar. He did enjoy some outdoor activities, particularly horseback riding. He was in college when you were born, majoring in music. He reported no medical problems.

Mother: Your birth mother was a single, white, Protestant young woman who was twenty years old at the time of your birth. She had auburn hair, brown eyes, and freckles. She was five-foot-four and weighed 145 prior to pregnancy. She was described by friends as warm, giving, and responsive. She also had a strong interest in music and art and played the piano. At the time of your birth she was a sophomore in college, also majoring in music. She wanted to become a concert pianist. Learning and accomplishment came easily to her. Her health problems included eye correction for nearsightedness and moderate difficulties with allergies.

Penny was overwhelmed with the similarities. When she joined her new family at two years of age she was the only adopted child in the house. She grew up with a loving, gracious family of light-complexioned blonds, even down to their blond cocker spaniel. As she grew into adolescence the differences widened. Her two sisters and brother all grew to over five-foot-nine and never struggled with problems of being "short and fat." Her own perceptions of herself made her wonder if she really "fit" in this family.

As is the case with many adopted people, Penny's perceived lack of similarities was the significant motivator in her birth search. Because she resembled no one in the household, she felt a sense of frustration, embarrassment, and insecurity.

The driving desire to find a genetic similarity was the only thing that encouraged Penny during the ten months it took to receive information:

> For the first time in my life, I felt physically attached to someone. I look like both my father and mother, suffer with her allergy problems, and now understand why I have such an interest in music. My adoptive family are all sports enthusiasts and I never could get interested. I am not such an oddity after all. In many ways, I am like my birth parents.
>
> My reason for the search was not to hurt my relationship with my parents. They are fantastic. I just wanted to know who I looked like and who I acted like. I wasn't

interested in meeting them or even in seeing them. I just wanted to know if someone else out in this world looked like me. That information was all I needed to put my search and my questions to rest.

WHERE AM I ON SOMEBODY'S FAMILY TREE?

Connie was adopted at age four, and by the time she entered fifth grade, she was well aware of it. In fact, reminders of the difference followed her even into the classroom. Memories of confusion and pain from one particular school assignment still surface occasionally:

> I recall one afternoon when our teacher gave an assignment that set off questions no one had answered for me.
>
> "We're going to build a family tree," she told us. I want you to bring in your baby pictures and pictures of your grandparents, aunts, and uncles."
>
> *Baby pictures,* I remember crying inside. *Don't you know that some adopted kids don't have baby pictures? And besides, other than my sister, I don't know another person on this earth who has the same flesh and blood as I do!*
>
> I can remember the fear I felt. What reason could I give to my friends why I didn't have those pictures? No one had ever fully explained it to me.

It was at that point, Connie acknowledged, that early feelings of being terribly alone began to haunt her.

The block to her past seemed to immobilize Connie emotionally. She couldn't see any continuity from her past relationships to her future ones. As an adult, an overwhelming need to find her place in the narrative of a family's story persuaded her to seek information about her birth family. Did she have genetically related aunts and uncles, grandparents and great-grandparents? Who were they and what were they like?

Connie's search, which included a genealogical survey through historical records, satisfied her need. She found her place on her birth family tree.

A NEED TO FORGIVE

One of the most painful burdens adopted children carry is the reality of having been given away. "For adopted children, part of them is hurt at having once been relinquished. That part remains vulnerable to grief and anger for the rest of their lives."[3] Without assistance to deal with the anger and grief and move toward forgiveness, adopted people are likely to find bitterness a close companion in adulthood.

These issues moved Randy to unravel an unknown past. Her story of healing and completeness offers hope to those in similar situations.

> As I entered adolescence, damaging thoughts took root in my heart and mind. I convinced myself that since my family life was different from anyone else's I knew, I wasn't as good as the rest of my friends. Tremendous feelings of inadequacy barred me from trying new things or from branching out into friendships.
>
> By the time I was nineteen, I was still plagued by feelings of deep resentment. I had a lot of anger toward the parents who had rejected me as a two-year-old. I became more and more bitter all the time. I don't know how many times I thought to myself, *Mom and Dad, you left me. You were never there for me.*
>
> I felt stuck in a downward spiral of negativism that drained me of happiness and peace. I had to put the fragmented pieces of my life together.
>
> I know that from the beginning, my birth search was directed by God. As I searched through records in a large metropolitan county courthouse, a clerk volunteered to help.
>
> "This is highly unusual," she informed me. "Just two weeks ago, a man was in here looking for the same information. Over two months ago, a young woman asked me these same questions. I gave them this address."
>
> Out of the multitude of personnel at the courthouse, this clerk helped all three of us. That afternoon, I learned I had a birth sister and brother and had a way to make

direct contact with my family of origin.

Like many adopted kids, I manufactured fantasies about my birth parents. I hoped to see them as wealthy people who deeply regretted giving me away. As I stood on the front porch of a small house that summer day, looking at the disheveled woman who had given birth to me, all sorts of emotions welled up within me. I spent three hours with her. Our conversation was empty and strained. What I heard and saw jarred me to reality. It was obvious that alcohol still permeated this home, just as I had been told. When I walked out the door I left my fantasies behind.

The process of healing began that day as I encountered the desperate, tragic state of my birth family. Their lives were empty—ravaged by alcohol, drug abuse, and poverty. God had spared me such a life.

Compassion filled me. I did forgive those who had left me with so many missing pieces. Now I could go on with my life, stronger with the reality of what my life has become.

WHAT HAPPENS AS A RESULT OF THE SEARCH?

Randy, Connie, and Penny, like millions of adults who conduct successful searches for information about their past, experienced positive results. Studies conducted with adults adopted as children have found that some are able to resolve inner conflicts connected to their condition and circumstances. Others mention that they are free of emptiness created by an unknown past. They are more able to establish a sense of identity. Many adopted adults indicate that one of the strongest positive results is a new level of closeness and intimacy in their relationship with their adoptive parents.

A study of adopted people who had completed some portion of a birth search found that all respondents experienced considerable improvement in their lives as a result of changes brought about by their search. References to significant improvements in self-esteem, self-confidence, and assertiveness appeared frequently. Others reported that they had finally acquired feelings of connection, which had previously escaped them. Still others alluded to increased peace of mind, a sense of calmness, and a greater ability to handle and express feelings.[4]

WHY DO SOME ADOPTIVE PARENTS RESPOND NEGATIVELY TO THE SEARCH?

Although some parents understand the need for their adopted child to seek his or her roots, others react negatively and fearfully. For some parents, the probe into the past resurrects painful, dormant memories.

When Sandy's twenty-year-old daughter, Ali, approached her with the news that she wanted to find her birth parents, Sandy was devastated. Once again Sandy was reminded that she was different. Once again she suffered the distressing memories of her inability to conceive a child. Old, disturbing emotions surrounding her own infertility and inadequacy surfaced — ones that she thought were resolved long ago.

Sandy's halting response to Ali's question, "Will you help me?" was strained and cool.

"If I can find the time," was all she could muster.

Linda's negative response to her son Keith's interest in conducting a search was rooted in another cause. Years before, sitting in a counselor's office, she had asked about this very issue. She was told by the counselor, "If you are the right kind of mother, your child will never want to search."

Today, Keith had asked the question. Today, a crushing sense of failure as a mother consumed Linda. She simply couldn't support Keith's intentions. His request only confirmed her perceived deficiency as a parent.

Feelings of inadequacy and failure are two reasons parents do not assist in the process. The third is fear. Parents have two primary fears: (1) loss of the relationship with their adopted child, and (2) the potentially harmful impact of the discoveries on the young adult.

"Some adoptive parents feel threatened by the desire to search," commented an adoptive mother of eight. "They fear that they will lose their child's affection. They are apprehensive about encouraging the child's birth search due to the frightening possibility that the discovery could permanently dissolve their family relationship and leave them childless again."

Some young adults (eighteen to twenty-one) are still unrealistic about what they will discover. They expect to find out that their natural parents now "have it all together" and will welcome them with open arms. This rarely happens.

Another fear for parents is that the child's discovery of possible negative origins may have long-lasting effects, especially concerning identity and self-worth issues. If young adults discover the complete truth of their family of origin, it could escalate feelings of inadequacy and worthlessness. But for some, it is a risk that must be taken.

HOW PARENTS CAN RESPOND
TO THE NEED TO SEARCH FOR GENETIC ROOTS

When faced with the prospect of a son's or daughter's appeal for help, parents must choose whether or not to support it. Adoption specialists concur that the most healthy response, which will keep family communication open, is to provide support. Involvement is vital, although the level may vary.

The first step that adoptive parents must take in supporting their adult child's search, according to Lois Melina, is to grant permission. This means letting their child know that it's all right with them if the child decides to search. "Related to this," Melina writes, "is the sharing of information the adoptive parents have about the birth parents or the adoption. It is hypocritical for us to say it's okay with us if the adoptee searches, but withhold information that could assist her in the search."[5]

SUGGESTIONS FOR SUCCESS
Parents often ask for practical suggestions on how to deal successfully with birth search issues. The following suggestions are intended to provide insight and encouragement for families who have yet to confront the issue as well as those who are in the midst of assisting their adult child in a search.

1. A family must be comfortable with the reality of adoption.

They must be willing to understand and accept, without personal threat or guilt, the lifelong dynamics that appear, disappear, and reappear.

2. Parents should share information about the child's adoption early. They should disclose what information they do have on a gradually increasing basis.

3. Parents must realize that a lot of groundwork needs to be laid before the search begins. This can be accomplished by communicating as a family and through an adoption-sensitive counselor, if necessary. The adult child may open up a Pandora's box of painful uncertainties or shattering realities. Adoptive parents may be needed to pick up the pieces.

4. Parents should not fear sharing their own personal concerns with their adult child. Honesty builds a stronger foundation for any family dealing with these issues.

5. Parents can communicate specifically what they are willing to do to help in the search. From attending how-to workshops to thumbing through phone directories, adoptive parents can choose the level of assistance they agree to provide.

Conducting any portion of the birth search is usually a highly emotionally charged process for all parties involved. If it is handled with sensitivity and openness from all participants — the child and adoptive parents — it can be a time of growth for everyone. It can also be a time when the efforts of molding and shaping "the promise" throughout many years find their greatest, deepest, and most meaningful rewards.

SUMMARY

Some adopted children ask few questions about their past. Others, however, not only raise many questions but vigorously seek answers. For adoptive parents facing this issue in the life of their adult child, it helps to recognize several primary reasons why children search for their roots:

- To obtain medical information
- To make a connection with their family of origin
- To gain information because of a lack of parental

knowledge of or communication about the adoption circumstances

■ To answer the questions, "Who do I look like? Who do I act like?"

■ To find their place on a genetic ancestry tree

■ To find and forgive

Occasionally, adoptive parents experience emotional difficulty in supporting the search, usually for the following reasons:

■ Issues surrounding their own infertility

■ Feelings of failure as a parent

■ Fear of losing their child's affection

■ Fear that the adult child's discovery of such negative origins may have long-lasting effects, especially concerning identity and self-worth issues.

QUESTIONS FOR SMALL GROUPS

1. What changes or additions, if any, would you make to the reasons listed in this chapter for why adopted adults choose to begin a birth search?

2. As an adoptive parent, what are your personal feelings regarding the existence of your adopted child's genetic relatives?

3. In your opinion, how open can and should an adoptive family be toward this entire question of searching for genetic roots?

4. What can families do if their child wishes to meet his or her birth parents? How do you think you would feel?

5. As an adoptive parent, how willing are you to be involved in this process?

Notes

CHAPTER 1 — CHOOSING TO LOVE A STRANGER:
   UNIQUE CHALLENGES ADOPTIVE PARENTS MUST FACE
1. David Kirk, *Shared Fate*, rev. ed. (Port Angeles, WA: Ben-Simon Publications, 1984), page 2.
2. Kirk, page 3.
3. David Brodzinsky and Marshall Schechter, *The Psychology of Adoption* (New York: Oxford University Press, 1990), page 46.
4. Kirk, page 6.
5. For a discussion of rejection of differences versus acknowledgment of differences, see Kirk, page 44.
6. Kirk, page 46.

CHAPTER 2 — CREATING A FAMILY:
   HOW DO CHILDREN ENTER OUR HOMES, AND WHO ARE THEY?
1. Angela Hunt, *The Adoption Option* (Wheaton, IL: Victor Books, 1989), page 24.
2. Linda Katz, "Parental Stress and Factors for Success in Older Child Adoption," *Child Welfare League of America*, vol. 65, no. 6, November/December 1986, page 571.
3. Patricia Baasel, "Genetics and Your Child," *Ours Magazine*, July/August 1988, page 13.
4. From a personal interview with Marietta Spencer at a conference of the

Adoptive Families of America, Los Angeles, California, 28 June 1992.
5. Baasel, page 15.
6. Dave Carder, et al., *Secrets of Your Family Tree: Healing for Adult Children of Dysfunctional Families* (Chicago: Moody Press, 1991), page 74.
7. Carder, page 74.

CHAPTER 3—WHAT BUILDS HEALTHY ADOPTIVE FAMILIES?
TEN CRITICAL SUCCESS FACTORS

1. Sula Wolff, *Children Under Stress* (Middlesex, England: Penguin, 1969), page 225.
2. Dr. Jerry Lewis, *How's Your Family?* (New York: Brunner/Mazel, 1989), page 13. The characteristics discussed under Factor One are adapted from this resource.
3. Lewis, page 48.
4. Linda Katz, "Parental Stress and Factors for Success in Older Child Adoption," *Child Welfare Journal*, vol. 65, no. 6, November/December 1986, page 574. Factors three, four, and five are adapted from this resource.
5. George Barna, *The Frog in the Kettle* (Ventura, CA: Regal Books, 1990), page 35.
6. Barna, page 35.
7. Quoted in Richard Lacayo, "Nobody's Children," *Time*, 9 October 1989, page 95.

CHAPTER 4—DEVELOPING A SUPPORTIVE ADOPTION ENVIRONMENT:
HOW TO PREPARE BIOLOGICAL CHILDREN, FAMILY, AND FRIENDS

1. Rita Law, quoted in Pat Johnson, *Speaking Positively* (Indianapolis: Perspective Press, 1992).
2. Margaret Ward and John Lewko, "Adolescents in Families Adopting Older Children: Implications for Service," *Child Welfare League of America*, vol. 66, no. 6, November/December 1987, page 540.
3. See Adele Faber and Elaine Mazlish, *Siblings Without Rivalry: How to Help Your Children Live Together So You Can Live Too* (New York: W. W. Norton, 1987), page 99.
4. Lois Melina, *Raising Adopted Children* (New York: Harper & Row, 1986), page 29.
5. This idea was provided by Dr. Jean-Pierre Bourguignon during a workshop at the Family Builder's Conference in South Carolina, May 1989.
6. David Kirk, *Shared Fate*, rev. ed. (Port Angeles, WA: Ben-Simon Publications, 1984), page 19.
7. Kirk, page 21.
8. Taken from *Language Guide on Adoption* (Cincinnati: Ohio Coalition for Adoption Reform, n.d.).
9. Lois Melina, "Guidelines for Explaining Adoption to Children Outside the Family," *Adopted Child*, vol. 10, no. 12, December 1991, page 1.
10. Cited by Lois Melina in "Teachers Need to Be More Sensitive to Adoption Issues," *Adopted Child*, August 1990.
11. See "Tough Questions that Deserve a Response," *Family Ties* (Lebanon, OH: Warren County Children Services, March/April 1992), page 2.

12. David Schooler, "So Fulfill the Law of Christ," sermon message presented to the Lebanon, Ohio, Church of the Nazarene during 1990.

CHAPTER 5 — ATTACHMENT:
HOW TO DEVELOP THE CRUCIAL BOND
1. Linda Bayless, *Assessing Attachment, Separation, and Loss* (Atlanta: Child Welfare Institute, 1990), page 3.
2. Bayless, page 3.
3. The long-range effects of attachments were presented by Dr. Vera Falhberg at the Adoptive Families of America National Conference in Los Angeles, 28 June 1992.
4. David Brodzinsky, Ph.D., Marshall D. Schechter, M.D., and Robin Marantz Henig, *Being Adopted: The Lifelong Search for Self* (New York: Doubleday, 1992), page 36.
5. Brodzinsky, et al., page 36.
6. Brodzinsky, et al., page 36.
7. Brodzinsky, et al., page 37.
8. Bayless, page 8.
9. From Dr. Kenneth Magid and Carole McKelvey, *High Risk: Children Without a Conscience* (New York: Bantam Books, 1987), page 257.
10. Bayless, page 28.
11. Jean-Pierre Bourguignon, *After Adoption* (Chicago: Illinois Department of Children and Family Services, 1988), page 19.
12. Some of the following material was presented at an adoptive parents support group, adapted from Wilfred Hamm, Thomas Morton, and Laurie M. Flynn, *Self-Awareness, Self-Selection and Success: A Preparation Guidebook for Special Needs Adoptions*, Janet Dinsmore, ed. (North American Council on Adoptable Children, 1985).
13. Connell Watkins, quoted in Magid and McKelvey, page 85.
14. Magid and McKelvey, page 86.
15. Adapted from Hamm, et al.
16. Magid and McKelvey, page 98.
17. Magid and McKelvey, page 91.
18. Magid and McKelvey, page 58.

CHAPTER 6 — BARRIERS TO ADJUSTMENT:
STRATEGIES TO EASE THE TRANSITION
1. See Jean-Pierre Bourguignon, *After Adoption* (Chicago: Illinois Department of Children and Family Services, 1988), page 19.
2. Claudi Jewett Jarrett, *Helping Children Cope with Separation and Loss* (Boston: Harvard Common Press, 1982), page 34.
3. The elements of the searching and bargaining stage are adapted from Jarrett, page 36.
4. Jarrett, page 36.
5. Bourguignon, page 19.
6. These suggestions are derived from several sources, including Lois Melina's *Raising Adopted Children* (New York: Harper & Row, 1986).

7. David Damico, *The Faces of Rage* (Colorado Springs: NavPress, 1992), page 35.
8. Damico, page 35.
9. Damico, page 34.

CHAPTER 7—HOW DO WE FEEL ABOUT ADOPTION?
   CRITICAL QUESTIONS FOR PARENTS AND CHILDREN

1. Quoted in David Brodzinsky and Marshall Schechter, *The Psychology of Adoption* (New York: Oxford University Press, 1990), page 19.
2. Brodzinsky and Schechter, page 19.
3. Brodzinsky and Schechter, page 19.
4. From a personal interview with David Brodzinsky in Los Angeles, California, 27 June 1992.
5. These advantages are adapted from Brodzinsky's work.
6. Brodzinsky and Schechter, page 23.
7. Brodzinsky and Schechter, page 20.
8. From a personal interview with David Brodzinsky.
9. Brodzinsky interview.
10. The developmental issues discussed in this chapter are adapted from resources created by the Parenthesis Project of Columbus, Ohio (P.O. Box 02265, Columbus, OH 43202).
11. Lois Melina, *Raising Adopted Children* (New York: Harper & Row, 1986), page 63.
12. Brodzinsky and Schechter, page 13.
13. Brodzinsky and Schechter, page 13.
14. L. M. Singer, et al., "Children's Belief About Adoption: A Developmental Study," *Journal of Applied Developmental Psychology*, no. 3 (1982), pages 284-94.
15. Elaine Frank, MSW, for the National Adoption Information Clearinghouse (Washington, DC: U.S. Department of Health and Human Services).
16. From Judy Emig's work for the Parenthesis Post Adoption Project.
17. Jill Krementz, *How It Feels to Be Adopted* (New York: Alfred A. Knopf, 1985), page 101.

CHAPTER 8—TALKING TO CHILDREN ABOUT ADOPTION:
   WHEN AND HOW

1. Quoted in Carolyn Jabs, "Adoption: When and What to Tell a Child," *Working Woman*, April 1991, page 46.
2. Quoted in Jabs, page 45.
3. Quoted in Jabs, page 46.
4. Quoted in Jabs, page 49.
5. See John and Jean Pardeck, "Bibliotherapy for Children in Foster Care and Adoption," *Child Welfare Journal*, vol. 66, no. 3, May/June 1987, page 271. Material on bibliotherapy in this chapter is adapted from this resource.
6. Pardeck, page 272.
7. From a video presentation by Jean-Pierre Bourguignon and Kenneth

Watson, *After Adoption* (Chicago: Illinois Department of Children and Family Services, 1988).
8. Hilary Beste and Rebecca Richardson, "Developing a Life Story Book Program for Foster Children," *Child Welfare Journal*, vol. 60, no. 8, September/October 1981.
9. Marian Parker, "Making a Child's Life Book," a workshop presented through the Ohio Regional Training Center, June 1988.
10. For information on constructing a genogram, contact your local library.
11. From a personal interview with Deborah Joy.

CHAPTER 9—CREATING A NURTURING FAMILY: GIVING OUR CHILDREN WHAT THEY NEED
1. Gary Smalley and John Trent, *The Gift of Honor* (Nashville, TN: Thomas Nelson Publishers, 1987), page 89.
2. Smalley and Trent, page 101.
3. David Damico, *The Faces of Rage* (Colorado Springs: NavPress, 1992), page 51.
4. From a personal interview with Dr. John Trent in Cincinnati, Ohio, November 1990.
5. Gary Smalley and John Trent, *The Blessing* (Nashville: Thomas Nelson Publishers, 1986), page 27.
6. Material in this section is adapted from a message by David Schooler, delivered to the West Carrollton, Ohio, Church of the Nazarene, May 1992.
7. Quoted from 1 Corinthians 13:4-8, *The New American Standard Bible*, © 1977 The Lockman Foundation.

CHAPTER 10—WHAT'S INSIDE AN ADOPTED ADOLESCENT? HELPING OUR TEENS RESOLVE FIVE PAINFUL ISSUES
1. The common adoption issues discussed in this chapter are adapted from resources received from the Parenthesis Post Adoption Project of Columbus, Ohio. For more information, write to them at: P.O. Box 02265, Columbus, OH 43202. The Parenthesis organization has been recognized for its progressive work with adopted teens.
2. Dr. Alan Dupre-Clark, "Identify Main Adoption Issues," *The Adoption Network Newsletter*, vol. 6, no. 1, January 1992. Published by the Parenthesis Family Advocates of Columbus, Ohio.
3. Betsy Keefer conducts support groups for adopted adolescents. For more information, contact the Parenthesis Post Adoption Project at the address listed above.
4. David Brodzinsky, Ph.D., Marshall D. Schechter, M.D., and Robin Marantz Henig, *Being Adopted: The Lifelong Search for Self* (New York: Doubleday, 1992), page 107.
5. Brodzinsky, et al., page 22.

CHAPTER 11—TRANSCULTURAL ADOPTION: PREPARING FOR SPECIAL CHALLENGES
1. Joyce Ladner, *Mixed Families: Adopting Across Racial Boundaries* (Garden

City, NY: Anchor Press, Doubleday, 1977), page 40.
2. From a personal interview with Pam Severs.
3. Severs interview.
4. This material is used by permission. Pamela Severs conducts workshops for families dealing with transcultural issues. She may be contacted by writing to her at: 1005 Rutland Way, Worthington, OH 43085.
5. Lois Melina, "Racial Identity Develops in Preschool Years," *Adopted Child,* vol. 2, no. 7, July 1983, page 2.
6. Melina, page 2.
7. David Brodzinsky, Ph.D., et al., *Being Adopted: The Lifelong Search for Self* (New York: Doubleday, 1992), page 62.
8. Used by permission of Pamela Severs.
9. The following suggestions have been adapted from Kathryn Donley of the New York Spaulding for Children.
10. Adapted from a tape by Lois Melina, "Raising a Child of a Different Race or Ethnic Background."

CHAPTER 12 — SEARCHING FOR A PAST:
WHY ADOPTED CHILDREN SEEK THEIR ROOTS
AND HOW PARENTS CAN RESPOND

1. David Brodzinsky and Marshall Schechter, *The Psychology of Adoption* (New York: Oxford University Press, 1990), page 69.
2. Brodzinsky and Schechter, page 318.
3. Robin Heng, "Chosen and Given," *New York Times Sunday Supplement,* 11 November 1988.
4. Adapted from Brodzinsky and Schechter, page 70.
5. Lois Melina, *Raising Adopted Children* (New York: Harper & Row, 1986), page 163.

Author

Jayne Schooler is the Adoption Coordinator for Warren County Children Services in Lebanon, Ohio. She has been involved with this agency since 1981, first as a foster parent, then as an adoptive parent, and later as a staff member. In 1983 Jayne and her husband, David, adopted their sixteen-year-old foster son, Ray.

In addition to her agency duties, Jayne conducts workshops for the Institute of Human Services, the training arm of the Ohio Department of Human Services. Her workshop emphasis is directed toward the training needs of foster and adoptive parents.

Jayne has participated in the development of curricula for foster and adoptive parents, which is used statewide. She has written over 125 articles that have been published in local, regional, and national magazines.

Jayne is a graduate of Cedarville College in Cedarville, Ohio.